Book 2 – Economics

SCHWESERNOTES™ 2011 CFA LEVEL 1 BOOK 2: ECONOMICS

©2010 Kaplan, Inc. All rights reserved.

Published in 2010 by Kaplan, Inc.

Printed in the United States of America.

ISBN: 978-1-4277-2741-1 / 1-4277-2741-4

PPN: 3200-0064

READINGS AND LEARNING OUTCOME STATEMENTS

READINGS

The following material is a review of the Economics principles designed to address the learning outcome statements set forth by CFA Institute.

STUDY SESSION 4 READING ASSIGNMENTS

Economics, CFA Program Curriculum, Volume 2 (CFA Institute, 2011)

STUDY SESSION 5 READING ASSIGNMENTS

Economics, CFA Program Curriculum, Volume 2 (CFA Institute, 2011)

STUDY SESSION 6 READING ASSIGNMENTS

Economics, CFA Program Curriculum, Volume 2 (CFA Institute, 2011)

Learning Outcome Statements (LOS)

Study Session 4

The topical coverage corresponds with the following CFA Institute assigned reading:

13. Elasticity

The candidate should be able to:

a. calculate and interpret the elasticities of demand (price elasticity, cross elasticity, and income elasticity) and the elasticity of supply, and discuss the factors that influence each measure. (page 10)

b. calculate elasticities on a straight-line demand curve, differentiate among elastic, inelastic, and unit elastic demand, and describe the relation between price elasticity of demand and total revenue. (page 16)

The topical coverage corresponds with the following CFA Institute assigned reading:

14. Efficiency and Equity

The candidate should be able to:

a. explain the various means of markets to allocate resources, describe marginal benefit and marginal cost, and demonstrate why the efficient quantity occurs when marginal benefit equals marginal cost. (page 21)

b. distinguish between the price and the value of a product and explain the demand curve and consumer surplus. (page 23)

c. distinguish between the cost and the price of a product and explain the supply curve and producer surplus. (page 24)

d. discuss the relationship between consumer surplus, producer surplus, and equilibrium. (page 25)

e. explain 1) how efficient markets ensure optimal resource utilization and 2) the obstacles to efficiency and the resulting underproduction or overproduction, including the concept of deadweight loss. (page 25)

f. explain the two groups of ideas about the fairness principle (utilitarianism and the symmetry principle) and discuss the relation between fairness and efficiency. (page 28)

The topical coverage corresponds with the following CFA Institute assigned reading:

15. Markets in Action

The candidate should be able to:

a. explain market equilibrium, distinguish between long-term and short-term effects of outside shocks, and describe the effects of rent ceilings on the existence of black markets in the housing sector and on the market's efficiency. (page 35)

b. describe labor market equilibrium and explain the effects and inefficiencies of a minimum wage above the equilibrium wage. (page 38)

c. explain the impact of taxes on supply, demand, and market equilibrium, and describe tax incidence and its relation to demand and supply elasticity. (page 39)

d. discuss the impact of subsidies, quotas, and markets for illegal goods on demand, supply, and market equilibrium. (page 42)

The topical coverage corresponds with the following CFA Institute assigned reading:

16. Organizing Production

The candidate should be able to:

a. explain the types of opportunity cost and their relation to economic profit, and calculate economic profit. (page 50)

b. discuss a firm's constraints and their impact on achievability of maximum profit. (page 51)

c. differentiate between technological efficiency and economic efficiency and calculate economic efficiency of various firms under different scenarios. (page 52)

d. explain command systems and incentive systems to organize production, the principal-agent problem, and measures a firm uses to reduce the principal-agent problem. (page 53)

e. describe the different types of business organization and the advantages and disadvantages of each. (page 54)

f. calculate and interpret the four-firm concentration ratio and the Herfindahl-Hirschman Index, and discuss the limitations of concentration measures. (page 55)

g. explain why firms are often more efficient than markets in coordinating economic activity. (page 56)

The topical coverage corresponds with the following CFA Institute assigned reading:

17. Output and Costs

The candidate should be able to:

a. differentiate between short-run and long-run decision time frames. (page 63)

b. describe and explain the relations among total product of labor, marginal product of labor, and average product of labor, and describe increasing and decreasing marginal returns. (page 63)

c. distinguish among total cost (including both fixed cost and variable cost), marginal cost, and average cost, and explain the relations among the various cost curves. (page 65)

d. explain the firm's production function, its properties of diminishing returns and diminishing marginal product of capital, the relation between short-run and long-run costs, and how economies and diseconomies of scale affect long-run costs. (page 69)

STUDY SESSION 5

The topical coverage corresponds with the following CFA Institute assigned reading:

18. Perfect Competition

The candidate should be able to:

a. describe the characteristics of perfect competition, explain why firms in a perfectly competitive market are price takers, and differentiate between market and firm demand curves. (page 77)

b. determine the profit maximizing (loss minimizing) output for a perfectly competitive firm, and explain marginal cost, marginal revenue, and economic profit and loss. (page 78)

   c.   describe a perfectly competitive firm's short-run supply curve and explain the impact of changes in demand, entry and exit of firms, and changes in plant size on the long-run equilibrium. (page 80)

   d.   discuss how a permanent change in demand or changes in technology affect price, output, and economic profit. (page 82)

The topical coverage corresponds with the following CFA Institute assigned reading:

19. **Monopoly**

The candidate should be able to:

   a.   describe the characteristics of a monopoly, including factors that allow a monopoly to arise, and monopoly price-setting strategies. (page 90)

   b.   explain the relation between price, marginal revenue, and elasticity for a monopoly, and determine a monopoly's profit-maximizing price and quantity. (page 91)

   c.   explain price discrimination and why perfect price discrimination is efficient. (page 92)

   d.   explain how consumer and producer surplus are redistributed in a monopoly, including the occurrence of deadweight loss and rent seeking. (page 93)

   e.   explain the potential gains from monopoly and the regulation of a natural monopoly. (page 94)

The topical coverage corresponds with the following CFA Institute assigned reading:

20. **Monopolistic Competition and Oligopoly**

The candidate should be able to:

   a.   describe the characteristics of monopolistic competition and an oligopoly. (page 101)

   b.   determine the profit-maximizing (loss-minimizing) output under monopolistic competition, explain why long-run economic profit under monopolistic competition is zero, and determine if monopolistic competition is efficient. (page 102)

   c.   compare and contrast monopolistic competition and perfect competition. (page 102)

   d.   explain the importance of innovation, product development, advertising, and branding under monopolistic competition. (page 104)

   e.   explain the kinked demand curve model and the dominant firm model, and determine the profit-maximizing (loss-minimizing) output under each model. (page 105)

   f.   describe oligopoly games including the Prisoners' Dilemma. (page 106)

The topical coverage corresponds with the following CFA Institute assigned reading:

21. **Markets for Factors of Production**

The candidate should be able to:

   a.   explain why demand for the factors of production is called derived demand, differentiate between marginal revenue and marginal revenue product (MRP), and describe how the MRP determines the demand for labor and the wage rate. (page 113)

   b.   describe the factors that cause changes in the demand for labor and the factors that determine the elasticity of the demand for labor. (page 114)

   c.   describe the factors determining the supply of labor, including the substitution and income effects, and discuss the factors related to changes in the supply of labor, including capital accumulation. (page 115)

d. describe the effects on wages of labor unions and of a monopsony and explain the possible consequences for a market that offers an efficient wage. (page 116)

e. differentiate between physical capital and financial capital and explain the relation between the demand for physical capital and the demand for financial capital. (page 118)

f. explain the factors that influence the demand and supply of capital. (page 118)

g. differentiate between renewable and nonrenewable natural resources and describe the supply curve for each. (page 120)

h. differentiate between economic rent and opportunity costs. (page 121)

The topical coverage corresponds with the following CFA Institute assigned reading:

22. **Monitoring Jobs and the Price Level**

The candidate should be able to:

a. define an unemployed person and interpret the main labor market indicators. (page 128)

b. define aggregate hours and real wage rates and explain their relation to gross domestic product (GDP). (page 129)

c. explain the types of unemployment, full employment, the natural rate of unemployment, and the relation between unemployment and real GDP. (page 129)

d. explain and calculate the consumer price index (CPI) and the inflation rate, describe the relation between the CPI and the inflation rate, and explain the main sources of CPI bias. (page 130)

The topical coverage corresponds with the following CFA Institute assigned reading:

23. **Aggregate Supply and Aggregate Demand**

The candidate should be able to:

a. explain the factors that influence real GDP and long-run and short-run aggregate supply, explain movement along the long-run and short-run aggregate supply curves (LAS and SAS), and discuss the reasons for changes in potential GDP and aggregate supply. (page 139)

b. explain the components of and the factors that affect real GDP demanded, describe the aggregate demand curve and why it slopes downward, and explain the factors that can change aggregate demand. (page 142)

c. differentiate between short-run and long-run macroeconomic equilibrium and explain how economic growth, inflation, and changes in aggregate demand and supply influence the macroeconomic equilibrium. (page 143)

d. compare and contrast the classical, Keynesian, and monetarist schools of macroeconomics. (page 146)

STUDY SESSION 6

The topical coverage corresponds with the following CFA Institute assigned reading:

24. **Money, the Price Level, and Inflation**

The candidate should be able to:

a. explain the functions of money. (page 151)

b. describe the components of the M1 and M2 measures of money and discuss why checks and credit cards are not counted as money. (page 151)

c. describe the economic functions of and differentiate among the various depository institutions and explain the impact of financial regulation, deregulation, and innovation. (page 152)

d. explain the goals of the U.S. Federal Reserve (Fed) in conducting monetary policy and how the Fed uses its policy tools to control the quantity of money, and describe the assets and liabilities on the Fed's balance sheet. (page 154)

e. discuss the creation of money, including the role played by excess reserves, and calculate the amount of loans a bank can generate, given new deposits. (page 155)

f. describe the monetary base and explain the relation among the monetary base, the money multiplier, and the quantity of money. (page 155)

g. explain the factors that influence the demand for money and describe the demand for money curve, including the effects of changes in real GDP and financial innovation. (page 156)

h. explain interest rate determination and the short-run and long-run effects of money on real GDP. (page 157)

i. discuss the quantity theory of money and its relation to aggregate supply and aggregate demand. (page 160)

The topical coverage corresponds with the following CFA Institute assigned reading:
25. U.S. Inflation, Unemployment, and Business Cycles
The candidate should be able to:

a. differentiate between inflation and the price level. (page 167)

b. describe and distinguish among the factors resulting in demand-pull and cost-push inflation and describe the evolution of demand-pull and cost-push inflationary processes. (page 167)

c. explain the costs of anticipated inflation. (page 169)

d. explain the relation among inflation, nominal interest rates, and the demand and supply of money. (page 169)

e. explain the impact of inflation on unemployment and describe the short-run and long-run Phillips curve, including the effect of changes in the natural rate of unemployment. (page 170)

f. explain how economic growth, inflation, and unemployment affect the business cycle. (page 171)

g. describe mainstream business cycle theory and real business cycle (RBC) theory and distinguish between them, including the role of productivity changes. (page 172)

The topical coverage corresponds with the following CFA Institute assigned reading:
26. Fiscal Policy
The candidate should be able to:

a. explain supply side effects on employment, potential GDP, and aggregate supply, including the income tax and taxes on expenditure, and describe the Laffer curve and its relation to supply side economics. (page 179)

b. discuss the sources of investment finance and the influence of fiscal policy on capital markets, including the crowding-out effect. (page 181)

c. discuss the generational effects of fiscal policy, including generational accounting and generational imbalance. (page 182)

d. discuss the use of fiscal policy to stabilize the economy, including the effects of the government expenditure multiplier, the tax multiplier, and the balanced budget multiplier. (page 183)

e. explain the limitations of discretionary fiscal policy, and differentiate between discretionary fiscal policy and automatic stabilizers. (page 183)

The topical coverage corresponds with the following CFA Institute assigned reading:
27. Monetary Policy
The candidate should be able to:

a. discuss the goals of U.S. monetary policy and the Federal Reserve's (Fed's) means for achieving the goals, including how the Fed operationalizes those goals. (page 189)

b. describe how the Fed conducts monetary policy and explain the Fed's decision-making strategy, including an instrument rule, a targeting rule, open-market operations, and the market for reserves. (page 190)

c. discuss monetary policy's transmission mechanism (chain of events) between changing the federal funds rate and achieving the ultimate monetary policy goal when fighting either inflation or recession, and explain loose links and time lags in the adjustment process. (page 191)

d. describe alternative monetary policy strategies and explain why they have been rejected by the Fed. (page 192)

The topical coverage corresponds with the following CFA Institute assigned reading:
28. An Overview of Central Banks
The candidate should be able to:

a. identify the functions of a central bank. (page 198)

b. discuss monetary policy and the tools utilized by central banks to carry out monetary policy. (page 198)

The following is a review of the Economics principles designed to address the learning outcome statements set forth by CFA Institute®. This topic is also covered in:

ELASTICITY

EXAM FOCUS

Elasticity is a measure of the ratio of the percentage change in one variable to the percentage change in another variable. It is commonly used as a measure of how sensitive the quantity demanded is to changes in the price of a good. After learning all about price elasticity of demand, learn how to apply this concept to calculate and interpret the cross elasticity of demand, the income elasticity of demand, and the elasticity of supply. You must also gain a good understanding of the factors that influence a good's elasticity of demand and elasticity of supply.

LOS 13.a: Calculate and interpret the elasticities of demand (price elasticity, cross elasticity, and income elasticity) and the elasticity of supply, and discuss the factors that influence each measure.

The **price elasticity of demand** measures the change in the quantity demanded in response to a change in market price (i.e., a movement along a demand curve).

The formula used to calculate the price elasticity of demand is:

$$\text{price elasticity of demand} = \frac{\text{percent change in quantity demanded}}{\text{percent change in price}} = \frac{\%\Delta Q}{\%\Delta P}$$

where:

$$\text{percent change} = \frac{\text{change in value}}{\text{average value}} = \frac{\text{ending value} - \text{beginning value}}{\left(\dfrac{\text{ending value} + \text{beginning value}}{2}\right)}$$

 Professor's Note: It is customary to use average values when calculating percentage changes used in elasticity computations. This way a change from 8 to 10 and a change from 10 to 8 both result in the same percentage change of 2 / 9 = 22.2%. Use this method on the exam!

Figure 1 illustrates the general categories of price elasticity of demand. A discussion of each is presented in the following:

- If a *small* percentage price change results in a *large* percentage change in quantity demanded, the demand for that good is said to be *highly elastic*. Apples are an example of an elastic good. The absolute value of price elasticity is greater than one, meaning that the percentage change in Q is greater than the percentage change in P.

©2010 Kaplan, Inc.

- If a *large* percentage price change results in a *small* percentage change in quantity demanded, demand is *relatively inelastic*. Gasoline is an example of a relatively inelastic good. The absolute value of price elasticity is less than one, meaning that the percentage change in Q is less than the percentage change in P.
- A *perfectly elastic* demand curve is horizontal, and its elasticity is infinite. If the price increases, quantity demanded goes to zero.
- A *perfectly inelastic* demand curve is vertical, and elasticity is zero. If the price changes, there will be no change in the quantity demanded.

Figure 1: Price Elasticity of Demand

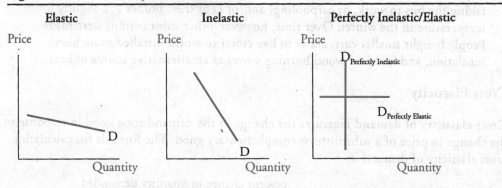

Example: Price elasticity

If the price of Product A is increased from $1.00 per unit to $1.10 per unit, the demand will decrease from 5.0 million units to 4.8 million units. Calculate the price elasticity of demand for Product A and determine if demand for Product A is elastic or inelastic.

Answer:

The percentage change in quantity = [(4.8 − 5.0)] / [(5.0 + 4.8) / 2] = −0.2 / 4.9 = −0.041 = −4.1%. The percentage change in price = [(1.10 − 1.00)] / [(1.10 + 1.00) / 2] = 0.10 / 1.05 = 0.095 = 9.5%. So, the price elasticity of demand for Product A is −4.1% / 9.5% = −0.43. Since the absolute value of the price elasticity of demand is less than 1.0, demand for Product A is *inelastic*.

Factors that influence the elasticity of demand are (1) the availability and closeness of substitute goods, (2) the relative amount of income spent on the good, and (3) the time that has passed since the price change of the good.

- *Availability of substitutes.* If good substitutes are available, a price increase in one product will induce consumers to switch to a substitute good. As such, elasticity of demand is determined, in part, by the availability of good substitutes. For example, the demand for gasoline is inelastic (less than one) because it has no practical substitutes, at least in the short run. On the other hand, the price elasticity for beef is high because there are many suitable substitutes, such as fish or chicken.
- *Relative amount of income spent on the good.* When the portion of consumer budgets spent on a particular good is relatively small, demand for that good will tend to be relatively *inelastic*. For example, consider toothpaste versus automobiles. Since people spend a relatively small amount of their incomes on toothpaste, a

10% increase in the price of toothpaste is not likely to change their consumption significantly, if at all. On the other hand, since the cost of an automobile is typically a significant proportion of a person's budget, a 10% increase in car prices may cause annual demand for cars to decrease significantly. Consumers can drive less and do more repairs to keep existing vehicles longer, or they can switch to alternative forms of transportation.

- *Time since the price change.* The price elasticity of demand for most products is greater in the long run than in the short run. Consider the situation in the 1970s when oil and gas prices rose significantly from historical levels. The short-run response was that people simply drove less (e.g., picking a closer vacation spot, taking the bus to work, or carpooling) and/or kept their homes at a slightly lower temperature in the winter. Over time, however, other substitutions were made. People bought smaller cars, chose to live closer to work, installed more home insulation, and installed wood burning stoves as an alternative source of heat.

Cross Elasticity

Cross elasticity of demand measures the change in the demand for a good in response to the change in price of a substitute or complementary good. The formula for calculating cross elasticity of demand is:

$$\text{cross elasticity of demand} = \frac{\text{percent change in quantity demanded}}{\text{percent change in price of substitute or complement}}$$

When two goods are reasonable substitutes for each other, cross elasticity is positive. On the other hand, cross elasticity is negative when two goods are complements. Complements are goods that are usually used together, so that an increase in the price of one would tend to decrease the quantity demanded of the other. An example would be automobiles and gasoline.

Example: Cross elasticity of demand (substitutes)

Suppose that the price of ice cream at your local ice cream parlor is $1.50 per scoop, and 600 scoops per day are sold. Now, assume that at the same parlor, the price of frozen yogurt increases from $1.25 to $1.75 per scoop. While nothing else has changed that could affect customers' buying patterns, the sale of ice cream increased from 600 to 750 scoops per day. Calculate the cross elasticity of demand of ice cream relative to frozen yogurt.

%ΔQ ice cream / %ΔP Yogurt

Answer:

The average quantity of ice cream demanded is (750 + 600) / 2 = 675 scoops, so the percentage change in the quantity of ice cream demanded is (750 − 600) / 675 = +22.2%. The average price for frozen yogurt is ($1.25 + $1.75) / 2 = $1.50 per scoop, so the percentage change in the price of frozen yogurt is ($1.75 − $1.25) / $1.50 = +33.3%. The cross elasticity of demand for ice cream relative to the price of yogurt is 22.2 / 33.3 = +0.67.

Professor's Note: For many people, ice cream and frozen yogurt are substitutes, so the cross elasticity of ice cream relative to the price of frozen yogurt is positive.

Example: Cross elasticity of demand (complements)

Suppose that the price of donuts is $0.50, and the local donut shop serves 800 donuts per day. At the same donut shop, the price of coffee is increased from $0.75 to $1.25 per cup. No other changes have occurred, and the number of donuts sold decreases to 600 per day. Calculate the cross elasticity of demand for donuts relative to the price of coffee.

$$\frac{\frac{600-800}{\frac{800+600}{2}}}{\frac{1.25-0.75}{1}} =$$

Answer:

The average quantity of donuts demanded is (800 + 600) / 2 = 700, so the percentage change in the quantity of donuts demanded is (600 – 800) / 700 = –28.6%. The average price for a cup of coffee is ($0.75 + $1.25) / 2 = $1.00 per cup, so the percentage change in the price of coffee is ($1.25 – $0.75) / $1.00 = 50%. The cross elasticity of demand for donuts relative to the price of coffee is –28.6 / 50 = –0.57.

 Professor's Note: Coffee and donuts are complements, so the cross elasticity of donut demand relative to the price of coffee is negative.

Income Elasticity

The **income elasticity of demand** measures the sensitivity of the quantity of a good or service demanded to a change in a consumer's income. The formula for income elasticity of demand is:

$$\text{income elasticity of demand} = \frac{\text{percent change in quantity demanded}}{\text{percent change in income}}$$

Inferior good < 1
necessarities 0 < x < 1
luxury > 1

Income elasticity of demand is related to the type of good being evaluated. <u>An inferior good has negative income elasticity.</u> As income increases (decreases), quantity demanded decreases (increases). Inferior goods include things like bus travel and generic margarine. In contrast, a **normal good** has positive income elasticity, which means that as income increases (decreases), demand for the good increases (decreases). Bread and tobacco are generally considered normal goods. Normal goods that have relatively low income elasticities (between 0 and +1) are considered *necessities*, while normal goods with high income elasticities (values greater than 1) are generally considered *luxury goods*.

Example: Income elasticity

Suppose that your income has risen by $10,000 from an initial rate of $50,000. Further, your consumption of bread has increased from 100 loaves per year to 110 loaves per year. Given this information, determine whether bread is a necessity or a luxury good.

$$\frac{\frac{10}{105}}{\frac{10,000}{55,000}} = 0.52$$

Answer:

Your average income is ($50,000 + $60,000) / 2 = $55,000, so the percentage change in income is ($60,000 − $50,000) / $55,000 = 18.2%. Similarly, the average quantity of bread demanded is (100 + 110) / 2 = 105 loaves, so the percentage change in the quantity of bread demanded is (110 − 100) / 105 = 9.5%. Thus, the income elasticity of bread is 9.5 / 18.2 = 0.52. Since its income elasticity of demand is less than 1, bread must be a necessity.

Elasticity of Supply

The **price elasticity of supply** is similar to the price elasticity of demand. It is a measure of the responsiveness of the quantity supplied to changes in price. That is:

$$\text{price elasticity of supply} = \frac{\text{percent change in quantity supplied}}{\text{percent change in price}} = \frac{\%\Delta Q}{\%\Delta P}$$

As shown in panel (a) of Figure 2 below, a perfectly inelastic (vertical) supply curve has an elasticity of supply of zero. Panel (b) illustrates a perfectly elastic (horizontal) supply curve with an elasticity of supply equal to infinity. For most goods and services, however, the elasticity of supply falls somewhere between these two extremes.

Figure 2: Inelastic and Elastic Supply

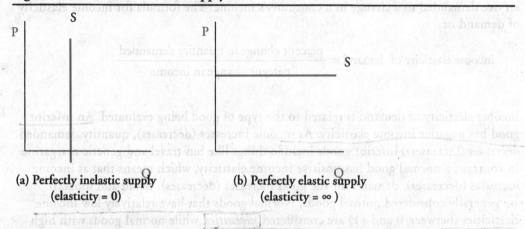

(a) Perfectly inelastic supply
(elasticity = 0)

(b) Perfectly elastic supply
(elasticity = ∞)

Example: Elasticity of supply

Suppose that the demand curve for coffee increases and that the equilibrium price for a pound of coffee increases from $8 to $10 per pound. At the new price, the quantity supplied increases from 100,000 kilograms per month to 120,000 kilograms per month, although the supply curve has not shifted. Calculate the elasticity of supply for coffee.

$$\frac{\frac{2\text{R}^{\prime\prime}}{110}}{\frac{2}{9}} \times \frac{9}{\downarrow} = \frac{9}{11}$$

Answer:

In this situation, the average quantity of coffee supplied is (100,000 + 120,000) / 2 = 110,000 kilograms, and the average price of coffee is ($8 + $10) / 2 = $9 per pound. So, the percentage change in quantity is (120,000 – 100,000) / 110,000 = 18.18%, and the percentage change in price is (10 – 8) / 9 = 22.22%. Thus, the elasticity of supply is 18.18 / 22.22 = 0.82.

Factors that influence the elasticity of supply are (1) the available substitutes for resources (inputs) used to produce the good and (2) the time that has elapsed since the price change.

Available resource substitutions. When a good or service can only be produced using unique or rare inputs, the elasticity of supply will be low. That is, the short-run supply curve may be nearly vertical for these goods. On the other hand, consider agricultural goods such as sugar and rice. These goods can be grown using the same land (resources), and the opportunity cost of substituting one for the other is nearly constant. As such, both of these products have highly elastic (nearly horizontal) supply curves.

Supply decision time frame. Three time-dependent supply curves must be considered when evaluating how the length of time following a price change affects the elasticity of supply: (1) momentary supply, (2) short-term supply, and (3) long-term supply.

1. *Momentary supply* refers to the change in the quantity of a good supplied immediately following the price change. When producers cannot change the output of a good immediately, the momentary supply curve is vertical or nearly vertical, and the good is highly inelastic. Grapes and oranges are examples of goods for which the quantity produced cannot be immediately changed in response to price changes. On the other hand, goods such as electricity have nearly perfectly elastic momentary supply curves. No matter what the demand for electricity, the amount provided can be changed without a significant change in price.

2. *Short-term supply* refers to the shape a supply curve takes on as the sequence of long-term adjustments are made to the production process. For example, manufacturing firms will adjust the amount of labor they use in response to a price change. The resulting increase or decrease in the cost of this input changes the shape of the supply curve. As time passes, additional adjustments may be made, such as technological innovations and training new workers, which will further change the shape of the supply curve, making it more elastic the longer the adjustment period.

3. *Long-term supply* refers to the shape of the supply curve after all of the possible ways of adjusting supply have been employed. This is usually a lengthy process. It may involve building new factories or distribution systems and training workers to operate them. Typically, long-term supply is more elastic than short-term supply, which is more elastic than momentary supply.

✱ supply curve elasticity
long term > short term > momentary

LOS 13.b: Calculate elasticities on a straight-line demand curve, differentiate among elastic, inelastic, and unit elastic demand, and describe the relation between price elasticity of demand and total revenue.

Price elasticity of demand is different at different points along a linear demand curve. Consider the demand curve presented in Figure 3.

Figure 3: Price Elasticity Along a Linear Demand Curve

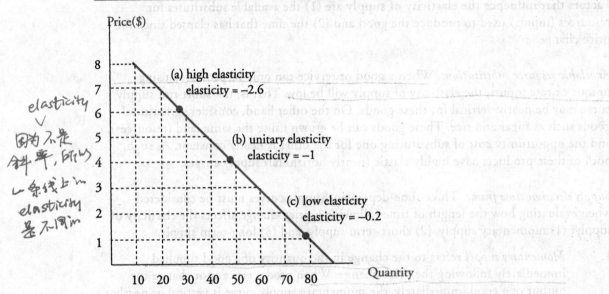

- At point (a), in a higher price range, the price elasticity of demand is greater than at point (c) in a lower price range.
- Price elasticity in the $6 to $7 range is [(20 – 30) / 25] / [(7 – 6) / 6.5] = –2.6.
- Price elasticity in the $1 to $2 range is [(70 – 80) / 75] / [(2 – 1) / 1.5] = –0.2.
- The elasticity at point (b) is –1; a 1% increase in price leads to a 1% decrease in quantity demanded. This is the point of greatest total revenue (P × Q), which equals 4.50 × 45 = $202.50.
- At prices less than $4.50 (inelastic range), total revenue will increase when price is increased. The percentage decrease in quantity demanded will be less than the percentage increase in price.
- At prices above $4.50 (elastic range), a price increase will decrease total revenue since the percentage decrease in quantity demanded will be greater than the percentage increase in price.

Thus, we can use a **total revenue test** to estimate elasticity of demand. If an increase (decrease) in price increases (decreases) total revenue, then demand is inelastic. If total revenue moves inversely to price (i.e., decreases with a price increase or increases with a price decrease), then demand is elastic at the current price.

> *Professor's Note: It is important that you notice that price elasticity of demand changes as you move along the demand curve. Elasticity is not simply the slope of the demand curve!*

KEY CONCEPTS

LOS 13.a

Price elasticity of demand refers to the responsiveness of quantity demanded to a change in price and is calculated as $\dfrac{\%\Delta \text{quantity demanded}}{\%\Delta \text{price}}$.

Demand is more elastic:
- the better the substitutes for the good.
- the greater the proportion of income spent on the good.
- in the long run (as more time has passed since the price change occurred).

Cross elasticity of demand refers to the responsiveness of the quantity demanded of a good to a change in the price of another good and is calculated as $\dfrac{\%\Delta \text{quantity demanded}}{\%\Delta \text{price of another good}}$.

Cross elasticity of demand is positive for goods that consumers consider substitutes for each other, and negative for goods that are complements (consumers tend to consume them together).

Income elasticity of demand refers to the sensitivity of the quantity demanded to a change in consumer incomes and is calculated as $\dfrac{\%\Delta \text{quantity demanded}}{\%\Delta \text{income}}$.

Income elasticity is negative for inferior goods and positive for normal goods, which are termed necessities if their income elasticity is between 0 and 1 and luxuries if their income elasticity is greater than 1.

Price elasticity of supply refers to the responsiveness of quantity supplied to a change in price and is calculated as $\dfrac{\%\Delta \text{quantity supplied}}{\%\Delta \text{price}}$.

Supply is more elastic in the long run (as more time has passed since the price change occurred). Supply is inelastic when the resources used to produce the good are rare or quite limited in available supply, and elastic when it is relatively easy to convert resources to the production of the good.

LOS 13.b

Along a straight line demand curve, demand is more (less) elastic at higher (lower) prices. Total revenue is maximized at the price and quantity where demand is unit elastic (price elasticity = –1) and so decreases with both price increases or price decreases from that level. When price is in the elastic (inelastic) region of the demand curve, a price increase will decrease (increase) total revenue.

CONCEPT CHECKERS

1. If the number of ice cream bars demanded increases from 19 to 21 when the price decreases from $1.50 to $0.50, the price elasticity of demand is:
   A. −5.
   B. −0.2.
   C. −0.1.

2. If quantity demanded increases 20% when the price drops 2%, this good exhibits:
   A. elastic, but not perfectly elastic, demand.
   B. inelastic, but not perfectly inelastic, demand.
   C. perfectly inelastic demand.

3. The primary factors that influence the price elasticity of demand for a product are:
   A. changes in consumers' incomes, the time since the price change occurred, and the availability of substitute goods.
   B. the proportions of consumers' budgets spent on the product, the size of the shift in the demand curve for a product, and changes in consumers' price expectations.
   C. the availability of substitute goods, the time that has elapsed since the price of the good changed, and the proportions of consumers' budgets spent on the product.

4. If a good has elastic demand, a small percentage price increase will cause:
   A. a smaller percentage increase in the quantity demanded.
   B. a larger percentage decrease in the quantity demanded.
   C. a larger percentage increase in quantity demanded.

5. The cross elasticity of demand for a substitute good and the income elasticity for an inferior good are:

	Cross elasticity	Income elasticity
A.	< 0	> 0
B.	< 0	< 0
C.	> 0	< 0

6. Income elasticity is defined as the percentage change in:
   A. quantity demanded divided by the percentage change in income.
   B. income divided by the percentage change in the quantity demanded.
   C. quantity demanded divided by the percentage change in the price of the product.

7. If quantity demanded for a good rises 20% when incomes rise 2%, the good is a(n):
   A. necessity.
   B. luxury good.
   C. inferior good.

8. When household incomes go up and the quantity of a product demanded goes down, the product is a(n):
   A. necessity.
   B. luxury good.
   C. inferior good.

9. If the price elasticity of demand is –2 and the price of the product decreases by 5%, the quantity demanded will:
   A. decrease 2%.
   B. increase 5%.
   C. increase 10%.

10. Which of the following is *most likely* a factor that influences the elasticity of supply for a good?
    A. The price of the productive resources used to produce it.
    B. The proportion of consumers' budgets spent on the good.
    C. The availability of substitute productive resources.

11. If the price elasticity of a linear demand curve is –1 at the current price, an increase in price will lead to:
    A. a decrease in total revenue.
    B. no change in total revenue.
    C. an increase in total revenue.

ANSWERS – CONCEPT CHECKERS

1. **C** If the number of ice cream bars demanded changes from 19 to 21 when the price changes from $1.50 to $0.50, the percentage change in quantity is (21 – 19) / [(21 + 19) / 2] = 10%, and the percentage change in price is (0.50 – 1.50) / [(1.50 + 0.50) / 2] = –100%. Thus, price elasticity = 10% / –100% = –0.1.

2. **A** If quantity demanded increases 20% when the price drops 2%, this good exhibits elastic demand. Whenever demand changes by a greater percentage than price, demand is considered to be elastic.

3. **C** The three primary factors influencing the price elasticity of demand for a good are the availability of substitute goods, the proportions of consumers' budgets spent on the good, and the time since the price change. If there are good substitutes, when the price of the good goes up, some customers will switch to substitute goods. For goods that represent a relatively small proportion of consumers' budgets, a change in price will have little effect on the quantity demanded. For most goods, the price elasticity of demand is greater in the long run than in the short run.

4. **B** If a good has elastic demand, a small price increase will cause a larger decrease in the quantity demanded. Demand is elastic when the percentage change in quantity demanded is larger than the percentage change in price.

5. **C** The cross elasticity of substitutes is positive, and the income elasticity of an inferior good is negative.

6. **A** Income elasticity is defined as the percentage change in quantity demanded divided by the percentage change in income. Normal goods have positive values for income elasticity, and inferior goods have negative income elasticity.

7. **B** A luxury good is a good for which the percentage increase in quantity demanded is greater than the percentage increase in income. A necessity is a good for which, when income increases by a given percentage, the quantity demanded increases, but by a smaller percentage. Since quantity demanded rose 20% when incomes rose 2%, the good in question is a luxury good.

8. **C** When household incomes increase and the quantity demanded of a good decreases, the product is an inferior good. Examples of inferior goods are bus travel and margarine (for some income ranges).

9. **C** If the price elasticity of demand is –2, and the price of the product decreases by 5%, the quantity demanded will increase 10%. The value, –2, indicates that the percentage increase in the quantity demanded will be twice the percentage decrease in price.

10. **C** The factors that influence the elasticity of supply are the possible resource substitutes and the time frame for the supply decision.

11. **A** On a linear demand curve, demand is elastic at prices above the point of unitary elasticity, so a price increase will decrease total revenue.

©2010 Kaplan, Inc.

EFFICIENCY AND EQUITY

EXAM FOCUS

The primary focus of this review is the efficient allocation of resources. The concepts of marginal benefit, marginal cost, consumer surplus, and producer surplus are all central to understanding the efficient allocation of productive resources. A basic understanding of the obstacles to the efficient allocation of resources and of the two schools of thought on economic "fairness" should be sufficient.

LOS 14.a: Explain the various means of markets to allocate resources, describe marginal benefit and marginal cost, and demonstrate why the efficient quantity occurs when marginal benefit equals marginal cost.

In a capitalist economy, most goods and services are **allocated by market price**. Those who are willing and able to pay the market price for various goods and services get those goods and services. There are, however, other methods for allocating scarce goods and services.

A *command system*, under which a central authority determines resource allocation, is used in centrally planned economies and is also used within firms and in the military.

Majority rule is also used to allocate resources. Governmental policies such as taxation and transfer payments are examples of this type of resource allocation.

Sometimes resources are allocated based on *personal characteristics*, such as race, religion, ethnicity, or sex. Other methods of allocating resources are *first-come-first-served*, *lotteries*, *contests*, and *force*, such as with extortion, theft, or warfare.

From an economic point of view, allocating resources, goods, and services by market price has some important advantages. When markets are functioning well, competition and allocation by price lead to an **efficient allocation of resources**, so that the **marginal benefit** to society just equals the **marginal cost** for the "last" unit of each good and service produced.

The "marginal" in marginal benefit and marginal cost refers to an additional unit, so the comparison between marginal benefit and marginal cost compares the benefit of one additional unit to the cost of producing that unit. As we shall see, the efficient allocation of a society's resources, and therefore the production of the efficient quantity of each good or service, is achieved when the benefit to society of producing one more unit just equals the cost to society of producing that additional unit. We measure the benefit to society as the value that a user places on the additional unit produced. We measure the cost to society as the opportunity cost of production (i.e., the value of other goods and services we must forego to produce the additional unit).

When markets function well, the demand curve for a good or service illustrates the (decreasing) value to consumers of additional units of a good or service, and the supply curve illustrates the opportunity cost of production of additional units of a good or service. We draw downward sloping demand curves to reflect the fact that each successive unit consumed will be less highly valued by consumers. We draw upward sloping supply curves to reflect the fact that the opportunity cost of producing additional units of a good increases as more and more resources are bid away from other productive uses to produce additional units of the good.

Given these interpretations of demand and supply curves, we can state that the **efficient quantity** of any good or service is the quantity where the demand curve and supply curve intersect. Figure 1 illustrates this result. If the economy produces less than 3,000 tons of steel, we have not maximized the benefit to society of steel production. The value that consumers place on additional units of steel is greater than the value consumers place on the other goods and services foregone to produce those units. Conversely, if the economy produces more than 3,000 tons of steel, each unit above 3,000 tons requires that society give up other goods and services more highly valued by consumers than the additional units of steel above 3,000 tons. As long as the demand curve represents the marginal benefit to society and the supply curve represents marginal cost to society, the benefit to society derived from producing steel is maximized at 3,000 tons.

Figure 1: Equilibrium and Efficient Quantity

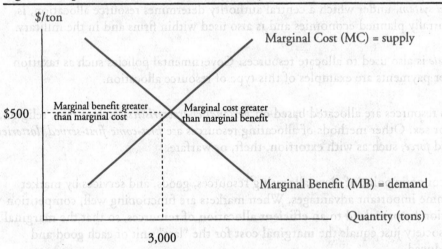

We refer to the quantity where the supply and demand curves intersect as the efficient quantity of production, and economists measure economic efficiency of production against this idealized solution. In a capitalist economy, each consumer's attempts to purchase that combination of goods that he values most highly, and each producer's attempts to maximize profits from production, result in **allocative efficiency**. Allocative efficiency is attained when the allocation of an economy's productive resources leads to the production of quantities of all goods and services that have the maximum total benefit to consumers. Contrast this with a centrally planned economy, where the government economic authority must determine the "right" quantity of every good or service produced in the economy, and you will understand the magnitude of the problem of providing the quantity of each good and service that will result in the greatest economic welfare for a country's citizens.

LOS 14.b: Distinguish between the price and the value of a product and explain the demand curve and consumer surplus.

The difference between the total value to consumers of the units of a good that they buy and the total amount they must pay for those units is called **consumer surplus**. In Figure 2, this is the shaded triangle. The total value to society of 3,000 tons of steel is more than the total amount paid for the 3,000 tons of steel, by an amount represented by the shaded triangle.

Figure 2: Consumer Surplus

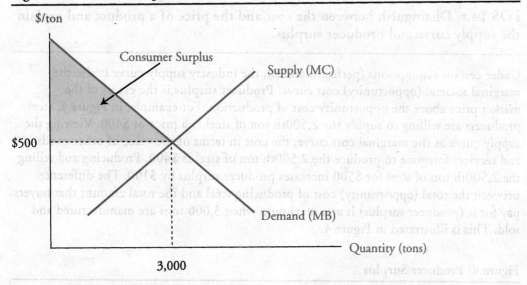

We can also refer to the consumer surplus for an individual. Figure 3 shows a consumer's demand for gasoline in gallons per week. It is downward sloping because each successive gallon of gasoline is worth less to the consumer than the previous gallon. With a market price of $3 per gallon, the consumer chooses to buy five gallons per week for a total of $15. While the first gallon of gasoline purchased each week is worth $5 to this consumer, it only costs $3, resulting in consumer surplus of $2. If we add up the maximum prices this consumer is willing to pay for each gallon, we find the total value of the five gallons is $20. Total consumer surplus for this individual from gasoline consumption is $20 − $15 = $5.

Figure 3: A Consumer's Demand for Gasoline

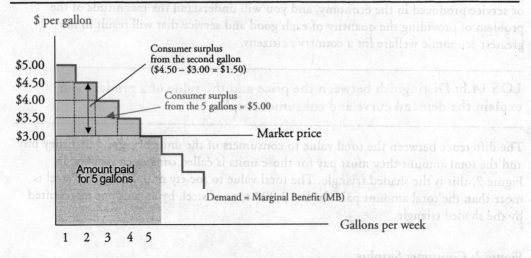

LOS 14.c: Distinguish between the cost and the price of a product and explain the supply curve and producer surplus.

Under certain assumptions (perfect markets), the industry supply curve is also the marginal societal (opportunity) cost curve. **Producer surplus** is the excess of the market price above the opportunity cost of production. For example, in Figure 4, steel producers are willing to supply the 2,500th ton of steel at a price of $400. Viewing the supply curve as the marginal cost curve, the cost in terms of the value of other goods and services foregone to produce the 2,500th ton of steel is $400. Producing and selling the 2,500th ton of steel for $500 increases producer surplus by $100. The difference between the total (opportunity) cost of producing steel and the total amount that buyers pay for it (producer surplus) is at a maximum when 3,000 tons are manufactured and sold. This is illustrated in Figure 4.

Figure 4: Producer Surplus

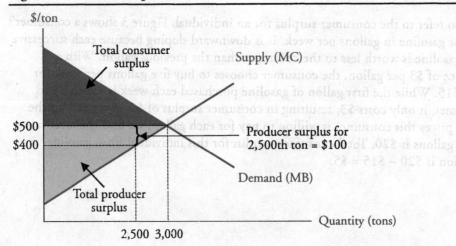

LOS 14.d: Discuss the relationship between consumer surplus, producer surplus, and equilibrium.

Note that the efficient quantity of steel (where marginal cost equals marginal benefit) is also the quantity of production that maximizes total consumer surplus and producer surplus. The combination of consumers seeking to maximize consumer surplus and producers seeking to maximize producer surplus (profits) leads to the efficient allocation of resources to steel production because it maximizes the total benefit to society from steel production. We can say that when the demand curve for a good is its marginal social benefit curve and the supply curve for the good is its marginal social cost curve, producing the *equilibrium quantity* at the price where quantity supplied and quantity demanded are equal maximizes the sum of consumer and producer surplus and brings about an efficient allocation of resources to the production of the good.

LOS 14.e: Explain 1) how efficient markets ensure optimal resource utilization and 2) the obstacles to efficiency and the resulting underproduction or overproduction, including the concept of deadweight loss.

Consider a situation where the allocation of resources to steel production is not efficient. In Figure 5, we have a disequilibrium situation where the quantity of steel supplied is greater than the quantity demanded at a price of $600/ton. Clearly, steel inventories will build up, and competition will put downward pressure on the price of steel. As the price falls, steel producers will reduce production and free up resources to be used in the production of other goods and services until equilibrium output and price are reached.

If steel prices were $400/ton, inventories would be drawn down, which would put upward pressure on prices as buyers competed for the available steel. Suppliers would increase production in response to rising prices, and buyers would decrease their purchases as prices rose. Again, competitive markets tend toward the equilibrium price and quantity consistent with an efficient allocation of resources to steel production.

Figure 5: Movement Toward Allocative Efficiency

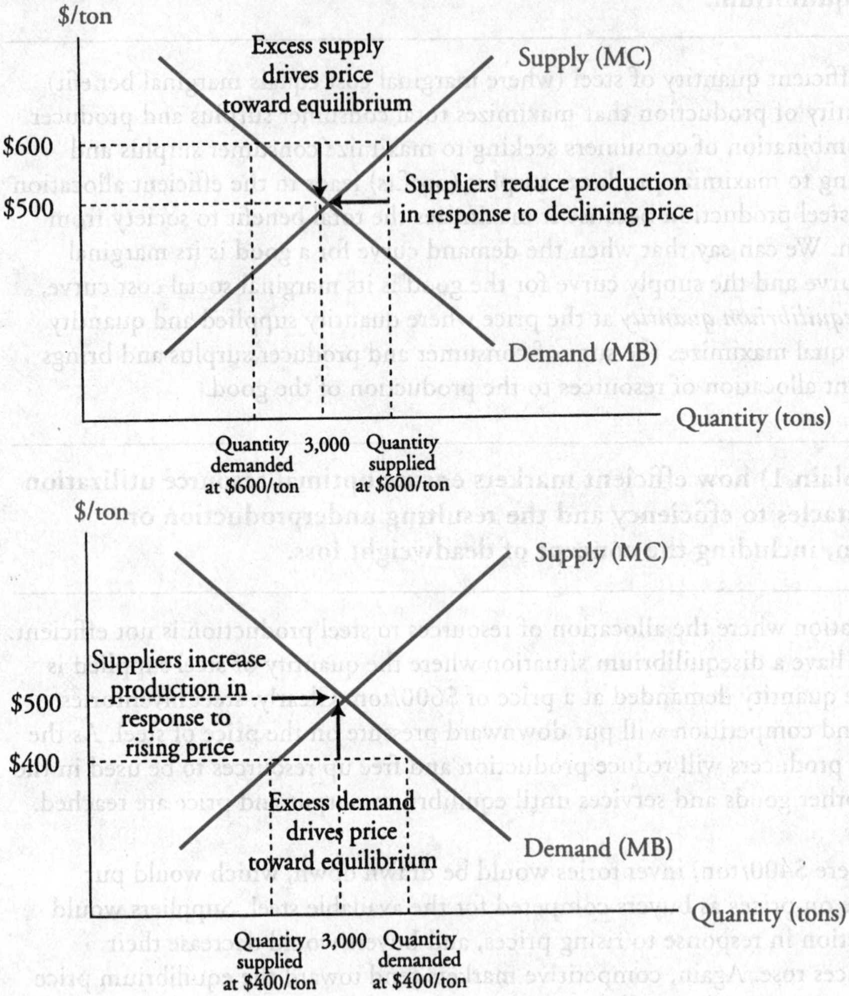

$/ton

Excess supply drives price toward equilibrium

Supply (MC)

$600

$500

Suppliers reduce production in response to declining price

Demand (MB)

Quantity (tons)

Quantity demanded at $600/ton   3,000   Quantity supplied at $600/ton

$/ton

Supply (MC)

Suppliers increase production in response to rising price

$500

$400

Excess demand drives price toward equilibrium

Demand (MB)

Quantity (tons)

Quantity supplied at $400/ton   3,000   Quantity demanded at $400/ton

Obstacles to Efficiency and Deadweight Loss

Our analysis so far has presupposed that the demand curve represents the marginal social benefit curve, the supply curve represents the marginal social cost curve, and competition leads us to a supply/demand equilibrium quantity consistent with efficient resource allocation. We now will consider how deviations from these ideal conditions can result in an inefficient allocation of resources. The allocation of resources is inefficient if the quantity supplied does not maximize the sum of consumer and producer surplus. The reduction in consumer and producer surplus due to underproduction or overproduction is called a **deadweight loss**, as illustrated in Figure 6.

Figure 6: Deadweight Loss

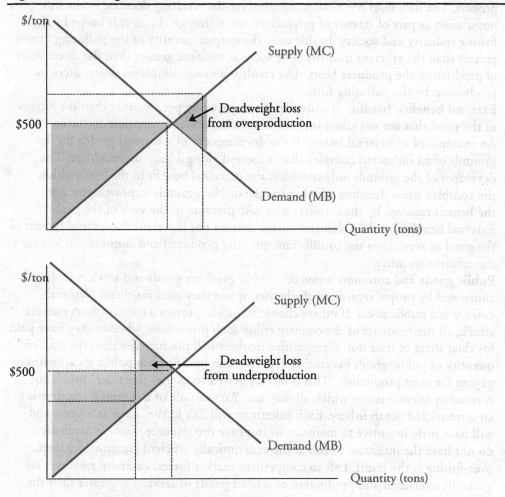

Obstacles to the efficient allocation of productive resources include:

- **Price controls,** such as price ceilings and price floors. These distort the incentives of supply and demand, leading to levels of production different from those of an unregulated market. Rent control and a minimum wage are examples of a price ceiling and a price floor.

- **Taxes and trade restrictions,** such as subsidies and quotas. *Taxes* increase the price that buyers pay and decrease the amount that sellers receive. *Subsidies* are government payments to producers that effectively increase the amount sellers receive and decrease the price buyers pay, leading to production of more than the efficient quantity of the good. *Quotas* are government-imposed production limits, resulting in production of less than the efficient quantity of the good. All three lead markets away from producing the quantity for which marginal cost equals marginal benefit.

- **Monopoly,** a situation where there is a single seller of a particular good or service. A single seller will choose a (profit-maximizing) quantity of production that is less than the efficient level of production.

- **External costs,** costs imposed on others by the production of goods which are not taken into account in the production decision. An example of an external cost is the cost imposed on fishermen by a firm that pollutes the ocean as part of its production process. The firm does not necessarily consider the resulting decrease in the fish population as part of its cost of production, even though this cost is borne by the fishing industry and society. In this case, the output quantity of the polluting firm is greater than the efficient quantity. The societal costs are greater than the direct costs of production the producer bears. The result is an over-allocation of resources to production by the polluting firm.

- **External benefits**, benefits of consumption enjoyed by people other than the buyers of the good that are not taken into account in buyers' consumption decisions. An example of an external benefit is the development of a tropical garden on the grounds of an industrial complex that is located along a busy thoroughfare. The developer of the grounds only considers the marginal benefit to the firms within the complex when deciding whether to take on the grounds improvement, not the benefit received by the travelers who take pleasure in the view of the garden. External benefits result in demand curves that do not represent the societal benefit of the good or service, so the equilibrium quantity produced and consumed is less than the efficient quantity.

- **Public goods and common resources.** *Public goods* are goods and services that are consumed by people regardless of whether or not they paid for them. National defense is a public good. If others choose to pay to protect a country from outside attack, all the residents of the country enjoy such protection, whether they have paid for their share of it or not. Competitive markets will produce less than the efficient quantity of public goods because each person can benefit from public goods without paying for their production. This is often referred to as the "free rider" problem. A *common resource* is one which all may use. An example of a common resource is an unrestricted ocean fishery. Each fisherman will fish in the ocean at no cost and will have little incentive to maintain or improve the resource. Since individuals do not have the incentive to fish at the economically efficient (sustainable) level, over-fishing is the result. Left to competitive market forces, common resources are generally over-used and production of related goods or services is greater than the efficient amount.

LOS 14.f: Explain the two groups of ideas about the fairness principle (utilitarianism and the symmetry principle) and discuss the relation between fairness and efficiency.

Two schools of thought regarding the fairness of the efficient allocation of resources in a competitive market focus on whether the results of the allocation of resources are fair and on whether the rules of the economic allocation of resources are fair.

One school of economic thought regarding efficient resource allocation is based on the general idea that it is not fair that individuals have dramatically different incomes. For instance, this school of thought contends that it is not fair that the CEO of a firm earns a significantly higher income than the common laborer. From within this framework, some early economists believed in the idea of utilitarianism—that the value of an economy is maximized when each person owns an equal amount of the resources. This early belief in utilitarianism has been proven wrong, but it warrants a closer look.

Utilitarianism is an idea that proposes that the greatest good occurs to the greatest number of people when wealth is transferred from the rich to the poor to the point

where everyone has the same wealth. Proponents of utilitarianism argue that
(1) everyone wants and needs the same things and has the same capacity to enjoy life,
and (2) the marginal benefit of a dollar is greater for the poor than the rich, so the
gain in marginal benefit to the poor from a transfer of wealth is greater than the loss
of marginal benefit to the rich. Since more is gained than lost, the end result after the
wealth transfer is that the total combined marginal benefit of the rich and the poor will
be greater.

The biggest problem with the utilitarian concept is the trade-off between fairness and
efficiency, resulting from the cost of executing the utilitarian wealth transfer. The most
important criticism of utilitarianism is based on the following argument. Wealth can be
transferred from high income earners to low income earners by taxing the high income
earners. This will cause the high income earners to work less, resulting in a less-than-
efficient quantity of labor being supplied. Further, the taxation of income earned from
capital investments will lead to reduced savings and investment. The end result is that
the quantities of both labor and capital will decrease, and the economy will shrink in
absolute size.

A second source of inefficiency associated with transferring wealth from the rich to the
poor through taxation is administrative costs. Taxation involves costs of collecting taxes
and auditing returns to enforce compliance. There is significant time and effort devoted
to calculating taxes by taxpayers. Welfare agencies have significant administrative costs,
which also reduce the amount of the actual transfer. All of the resources and labor used
in these activities could be used to produce other goods and services that have value to
consumers.

A second school of economic thought is based on the **symmetry principle**. The
symmetry principle holds that people in similar situations should be treated similarly. It
is basically a moral principle that advocates treating other people the way you prefer to
be treated. Economically speaking, this means equality of opportunity.

In *Anarchy, State, and Utopia* (1974), Robert Nozick argues that results are irrelevant
to the idea of fair resource allocation—fairness must be based on the fairness of the
rules. He suggests that fairness adhere to two rules: (1) governments must recognize
and protect private property, and (2) private property must be given from one party to
another only when it is voluntarily done. Rule (1) means that everything that is valuable
must be owned by individuals, and the government must enforce private property rights.
Rule (2) means that the only way an individual can acquire property is through an
exchange for something else that he owns (including his own labor).

Nozick argues that if these uniquely fair rules are followed, the result will be fair. It
doesn't matter if the whole economy is shared equally, as long as it is constructed by
the same individuals, each of whom provides services on a voluntary basis in exchange
for economic benefit. This is what is meant by symmetry—individuals get goods and
services from the economy that are equal in value to their contributions to the economy.

KEY CONCEPTS

LOS 14.a

Resources can be allocated by markets or by other means, including a command system, majority rule, contests, first-come-first-served, lotteries, personal characteristics, or force.

Marginal benefit is the benefit derived from consuming one additional unit of a good or service. Marginal cost, the cost of producing one more unit of a good or service, is considered an opportunity cost because it represents the value of the goods the productive resources used could produce in their next-highest-valued use.

Resources are efficiently allocated when each good or service is produced in a quantity for which the benefit to society of the last unit produced (its marginal benefit) just equals the costs to society of producing that unit (its marginal cost).

LOS 14.b

Consumer surplus is the difference between the total value consumers, or a consumer, place on the units of a good they consume and the total amount they must pay for it.

The demand curve for a good or service is the sum of all consumers' downward sloping marginal benefit curves.

LOS 14.c

The supply curve for a good or service is the sum of all producers' upward sloping marginal cost curves and represents the quantity that will be willingly produced and sold at different prices.

Producer surplus is the difference between the total cost of producing output and the total amount producers receive for it.

LOS 14.d

The quantity demanded just equals the quantity supplied at the equilibrium price. At this price and quantity, the sum of consumer surplus and producer surplus (total surplus) is at a maximum.

LOS 14.e

In the absence of impediments such as taxes, subsidies, price controls, trade restrictions, high transactions costs, common resource use, and monopoly, competitive markets and resulting equilibrium prices will result in an efficient allocation of resources and the production of the efficient quantities of goods and services that are not public goods.

A deadweight loss is the reduction in total surplus which results from producing either more or less than the efficient quantity of a good or service.

LOS 14.f

Utilitarianism is based on the goal of creating the greatest good for society and underlies the argument that wealth should be transferred from the rich to the poor (who presumably get more benefit from it).

The symmetry principle, the idea that people in similar circumstances should be treated similarly, underlies the idea of equality of opportunity and the conclusion that fair rules lead to a fair outcome.

CONCEPT CHECKERS

1. If a consumer is willing to pay $20 for a shirt but only has to pay $16, the $4 difference is:
    A. consumer surplus.
    B. consumer deficit.
    C. producer surplus.

2. The marginal benefit from consuming the third unit of a product is $12, and the marginal cost to the producer of the third unit is $8. Under these circumstances, which of the following statements is *most accurate*?
    A. Producer surplus is maximized.
    B. The efficient quantity is less than three.
    C. Producing and selling the third unit will increase efficiency.

3. The idea that a competitive market allocates resources fairly as long as the same rules apply to all participants is suggested by:
    A. utilitarianism.
    B. the fairness principle.
    C. the symmetry principle.

4. In an unregulated competitive market, which of the following conditions *most accurately* describes the condition that exists when the efficient quantity of a good or service is produced and consumed?
    A. Producer surplus is maximized.
    B. Consumer surplus equals producer surplus.
    C. The sum of consumer surplus and producer surplus is maximized.

5. Producer surplus is *best* defined as the:
    A. number of units by which the supply is greater than the quantity demanded by consumers.
    B. sum of the differences between the price of each unit of a good and its opportunity cost.
    C. amount by which the price of the next unit of a good exceeds the consumer's marginal benefit from the good.

6. Which of the following statements *most accurately* describes what will occur in an unrestricted economy when tastes change so that marginal benefit exceeds marginal cost at the current quantity produced and sold of a good or service?
    A. The quantity consumed will decrease.
    B. The quantity of the good or service produced will increase.
    C. The quantity of other goods and services produced will increase.

7. Which of the following is *least likely* an obstacle to the efficient allocation of resources?
    A. Price deregulation.
    B. Taxes, quotas, and subsidies.
    C. Public goods and common resources.

8.   As the demand (marginal benefit) curve becomes less elastic, if the equilibrium
      price and quantity remain unchanged, consumer surplus:
      A. decreases.
      B. increases.
      C. remains unchanged.

ANSWERS – CONCEPT CHECKERS

1. **A** If a consumer is willing to pay $20 for a shirt but only pays $16 for the shirt, the $4 difference is consumer surplus. The consumer surplus plus the market price equals the total value of the product to the consumer.

2. **C** When marginal benefit exceeds marginal cost, increasing the quantity of the good produced improves allocative efficiency.

3. **C** The symmetry principle holds that people in similar situations should be treated similarly. It implies that the market allocates resources fairly if the rules that markets operate by are equitable.

4. **C** When the efficient quantity is produced, the sum of consumer surplus and producer surplus is maximized.

5. **B** The sum of the differences between price and opportunity cost is producer surplus.

6. **B** In an unrestricted economy, the efficient quantity is the one for which the marginal benefit equals the marginal cost. When marginal benefit is greater than marginal cost at a given quantity, producers will produce more since consumers are willing to pay more than the cost of production.

7. **A** Price deregulation removes an obstacle to the efficient allocation of resources.

8. **B** Refer to Figure 4. You can see that the area of the triangle that represents consumer surplus increases as the steepness of the demand (marginal benefit) curve increases at a given equilibrium price and quantity.

Markets in Action

Exam Focus

This review examines how market equilibrium is affected by price ceilings, minimum wages, taxes, subsidies, quotas, and trade in illegal goods. For each of these you should know how supply, demand, and the resulting market equilibrium price and quantity are affected. It is important to understand why economists believe that, in general, interference with market forces causes economic inefficiency (an inefficient allocation of resources).

LOS 15.a: Explain market equilibrium, distinguish between long-term and short-term effects of outside shocks, and describe the effects of rent ceilings on the existence of black markets in the housing sector and on the market's efficiency.

Market equilibrium, as we saw in the previous topic review, occurs at the price where the quantity supplied is equal to the quantity demanded.

Outside shocks, such as natural disasters, can temporarily interrupt the supply of goods or services. In Panel (a) of Figure 1, this is shown as a shift to the left in the short-run supply curve. The *short run* is the period in which producers cannot adjust their capacity. Assuming the outside shock does not affect demand, the reduction in supply results in a higher equilibrium price and lower equilibrium output in the short run.

In the long term, when producers can adjust capacity, they find that the higher price is an opportunity to profit by increasing their output. The resulting higher output quantity drives the equilibrium price lower again. Other things equal, in the long run, both price and quantity can return to their equilibrium levels prior to the outside shock, as shown in Panel (b) of Figure 1.

Figure 1: Impact of an Outside Shock

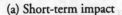

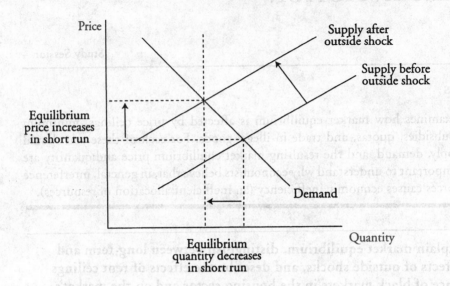

(a) Short-term impact

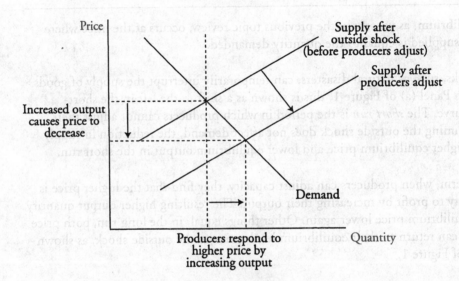

(b) Long-term impact

An example of a supply shock from a disaster is an earthquake that destroys a significant portion of the housing stock in an area. Initially, rents rise because of the decrease in supply. Over time, spare rooms and garages are converted to rentable housing and new units of housing are constructed in response to the price increase. This accounts for the increase in supply over time; prices eventually fall to prior levels as more supply is created. However, increasing rents often bring calls for authorities to intervene in the market by imposing price controls. Limiting how high rents can go decreases the incentive to create more housing units in the short run.

A **price ceiling** is an upper limit on the price which a seller can charge. If the ceiling is above the equilibrium price, it will have no effect. As illustrated in Figure 2, if the ceiling is below the equilibrium price, the result will be a shortage (excess demand) at the ceiling price. The quantity demanded, Q_d, exceeds the quantity supplied, Q_s. Consumers are willing to pay P_{WS} (price with search costs) for the Q_s quantity suppliers are willing to sell at the ceiling price, P_C. Consumers are willing to expend effort with a value of $P_{WS} - P_C$ in search activity to find the scarce good. The reduction in quantity exchanged due to the price ceiling leads to a deadweight loss in efficiency as noted in Figure 2.

Figure 2: Price Ceiling

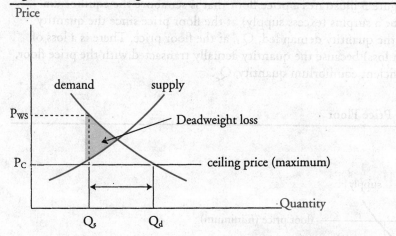

With an effective price ceiling, price is no longer an effective means of rationing the good or service. In the long run, price ceilings lead to the following:

- Consumers may have to wait in long lines to make purchases. They pay a price (an opportunity cost) in terms of the time they spend in line.
- Suppliers may engage in discrimination, such as selling to friends and relatives first.
- Suppliers "officially" sell at the ceiling price but take bribes to do so.
- Suppliers may also reduce the quality of the goods produced to a level commensurate with the ceiling price.

In the housing market, price ceilings are appropriately called **rent ceilings** or rent control. Rent ceilings are a good example of how a price ceiling can distort a market. Renters must wait for units to become available. Renters may have to bribe landlords to rent at the ceiling price. The quality of the apartments will fall. Other inefficiencies can develop. For instance, a renter might be reluctant to take a new job across town because it means giving up a rent-controlled apartment and risking not finding another (rent-controlled) apartment near the new place of work.

A **black market** refers to economic activity that takes place illegally. This includes selling goods at prices that exceed legally imposed price ceilings. Bribing a landlord to get a rent-controlled apartment is an example of black market activity. Another way for a landlord to charge rent that exceeds the rent ceiling is to "officially" rent at the ceiling, then charge excessive fees for items such as mailboxes, keys and locks, or window treatments.

A black market is generally inefficient because:

- Contracts are not as enforceable.
- The risk of prosecution increases the prices required by suppliers.
- Quality control deteriorates, which leads to more defective products.

LOS 15.b: Describe labor market equilibrium and explain the effects and inefficiencies of a minimum wage above the equilibrium wage.

A **price floor** is a minimum price that a buyer can offer for a good, service, or resource. If the price floor is below the equilibrium price, it will have no effect on equilibrium price and quantity. Figure 3 illustrates a price floor that is set above the equilibrium price. The result will be a surplus (excess supply) at the floor price since the quantity supplied, Q_s, exceeds the quantity demanded, Q_d, at the floor price. There is a loss of efficiency (deadweight loss) because the quantity actually transacted with the price floor, Q_d, is less than the efficient equilibrium quantity, Q_e.

Figure 3: Impact of a Price Floor

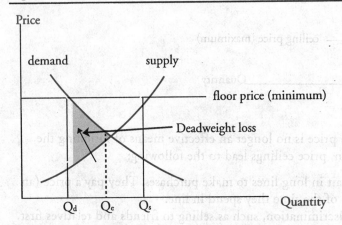

In the long run, price floors lead to inefficiencies:

- Suppliers will divert resources to the production of the good with the anticipation of selling the good at the floor price but then will not be able to sell all they produce.
- Consumers will buy less of a product if the floor is above the equilibrium price and substitute other, less expensive consumption goods for the good subject to the price floor.

In the labor market, as in all markets, equilibrium occurs when the quantity demanded (of hours worked, in this case) equals the quantity supplied. In the labor market, the equilibrium price is called the **wage rate**. The equilibrium wage rate is different for labor of different kinds and with various levels of skill. Labor that requires the lowest skill level (unskilled labor) generally has the lowest wage rate.

In some places, including the United States, there is a **minimum wage** rate (sometimes defined as a *living wage*) that prevents employers from hiring workers at a wage less than the legal minimum. The minimum wage is an example of a price floor. At a minimum wage above the equilibrium wage, there will be an excess supply of workers, since firms cannot employ all the workers who want to work at that wage. Since firms must pay at least the minimum wage for the workers, firms substitute other productive resources for labor and use more than the economically efficient amount of capital. The result is increased unemployment because even when there are workers willing to work at a wage lower than the minimum, firms cannot legally hire them. Furthermore, firms may decrease the quality or quantity of the nonmonetary benefits they previously offered to workers, such as pleasant, safe working conditions and on-the-job training.

LOS 15.c: Explain the impact of taxes on supply, demand, and market equilibrium, and describe tax incidence and its relation to demand and supply elasticity.

A tax on a good or service will increase its equilibrium price and decrease its equilibrium quantity. Figure 4 illustrates the effects of a *tax on producers* and of a *tax on buyers* (e.g., a sales tax). In Panel (a) the points indicated by P_E and Q_E describe the equilibrium prior to the tax. As a result of this tax, the supply curve shifts from S to S_{tax}, where the quantity Q_{tax} is demanded at the price P_{tax}.

The tax is the difference between what buyers pay and what sellers ultimately earn per unit. This is illustrated by the vertical distance between supply curve S and supply curve S_{tax}. At the new quantity, Q_{tax}, buyers pay P_{tax}, but net of the tax, suppliers only receive P_S. The triangular area is a **deadweight loss** (DWL). This is the loss of gains from production and trade that results from the tax (i.e., because less than the efficient amount is produced and consumed).

Note that in Panel (b), although the statutory incidence of the tax is on buyers, the actual incidence of the tax, the reduction in output, and the consequent deadweight loss are all the same as in Panel (a), where the tax is imposed on sellers.

The **tax revenue** is the amount of the tax times the new equilibrium quantity, Q_{tax}. Economic agents (buyers and sellers) in the market share the burden of the tax revenue. The **incidence of a tax** is allocation of this tax between buyers and sellers. The rectangle denoted "revenue from buyers" represents the portion of the *tax revenue* that the buyers effectively pay. The rectangle denoted "revenue from sellers" illustrates the portion of the tax that the suppliers effectively pay.

Figure 4: Incidence of a Tax on Producers and of a Tax on Buyers

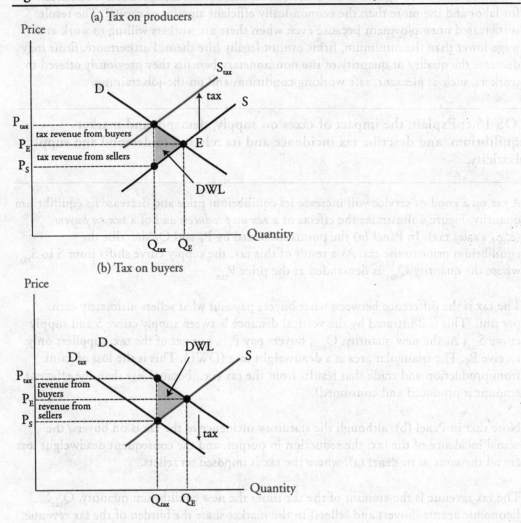

Actual and Statutory Incidence of a Tax

Statutory incidence refers to who is legally responsible for paying the tax. The **actual incidence of a tax** refers to who actually bears the cost of the tax through an increase in the price paid (buyers) or decrease in the price received (sellers). In Figure 4(a), we illustrated the effect of a tax on the *sellers* of the good as opposed to the *buyers* of the good (note that the price is higher over all levels of production—the supply curve shifts up). Thus, the *statutory incidence* in Figure 4(a) is on the supplier. The result is an increase in price at each possible quantity supplied.

Statutory incidence on the *buyer* causes a downward shift of the demand curve by the amount of the tax. As indicated in Figure 4(b), prior to the imposition of a tax on buyers, the equilibrium price and quantity are at the point of intersection of the supply and demand curves (i.e., P_E, Q_E). The imposition of the tax forces suppliers to reduce output to the point Q_{tax} (a movement along the supply curve). At the new equilibrium, price and quantity are denoted by P_{tax} and Q_{tax}, respectively.

The tax that we are analyzing in Figure 4(b) could be a sales tax that is added to the price of the good at the time of sale. So, instead of paying P_E, buyers are now forced to pay P_{tax}, (i.e., tax = $P_{tax} - P_E$). The *buyer* pays the entire tax (the statutory incidence). Since, prior to the imposition of the tax, their reference point was P_E, the *buyer* only sees the price rise from P_E to P_{tax} (the buyer's tax burden). Hence, the portion of the tax borne by buyers is the area between P_E and P_{tax}, with width Q_{tax}; this is the actual tax incidence on buyers.

Note that the supply curve in Figure 4(b) does not move as a result of a tax on buyers and that given the original demand curve, D, suppliers would have supplied the equilibrium quantity Q_E at price P_E. The result is that suppliers are penalized because they would have produced at the Q_E, P_E point, but instead produce quantity Q_{tax} and receive P_S. Hence, the portion of the tax borne by sellers is the area between P_E and P_S, with width Q_{tax}; this is the actual tax incidence on sellers. Note that we are still faced with the triangular deadweight loss.

> *Professor's Note: The point you need to know is that the actual tax incidence is independent of whether the government imposes the tax (statutory incidence) on consumers or suppliers.*

How Elasticities of Supply and Demand Influence the Incidence of a Tax

When buyers and sellers share the tax burden, the relative elasticities of supply and demand will determine the actual incidence of a tax.

- If *demand is less elastic* (i.e., the demand curve is steeper) than supply, *consumers will bear a higher burden*—that is, pay a greater portion of the tax revenue than suppliers.
- If *supply is less elastic* (i.e., the supply curve is steeper) than demand, *suppliers will bear a higher burden*—that is, pay a greater portion of the tax revenue than consumers. Here, the change in the quantity supplied for a given change in price will be small—buyers have more "leverage" in this type of market. The party with the more elastic curve will be able to react more to the changes imposed by the tax. Hence, they can avoid more of the burden.

Panels (a) and (b) in Figure 5 are the same in all respects, except that the supply curve in Panel (b) is significantly steeper—it is less elastic. Comparing Panel (a) with Panel (b), we can see that the portion of tax revenue borne by the seller is much greater than that borne by the buyer as the supply curve becomes less elastic. When demand is more elastic relative to supply, buyers pay a lower portion of the tax because they have the greater ability to substitute away from the good.

Notice that as the elasticity of either demand or supply decreases, the deadweight loss is also reduced. This is because fewer trading opportunities are eliminated by the imposition of the tax, meaning that it is more difficult for either demanders or suppliers to substitute away from the good. With less effect on equilibrium quantity, the allocation of resources is less affected and efficiency is reduced less.

Figure 5: Elasticity of Supply and Tax Incidence

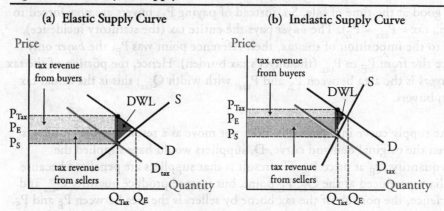

In Figure 6, we illustrate the result for differences in the elasticity of demand. In Panel (b), demand is relatively more inelastic, and we see that the size of the deadweight loss (and the decrease in equilibrium output) is smaller when demand is more inelastic. We can also see that the actual incidence of a tax falls more heavily on buyers when demand is more inelastic.

Figure 6: Elasticity of Demand and Tax Incidence

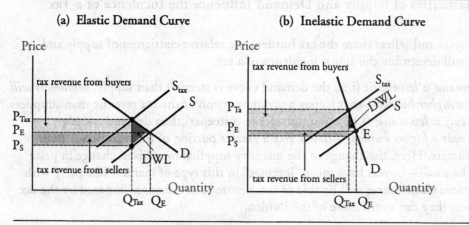

LOS 15.d: Discuss the impact of subsidies, quotas, and markets for illegal goods on demand, supply, and market equilibrium.

Subsidies are payments made by governments to producers, often farmers. The effects of a subsidy are illustrated in Figure 7, where we use the market for soybeans as an example. Note here that with no subsidies, equilibrium quantity in the market for soybeans is 60 tons annually at a price of $60 per ton. A subsidy of $30 per ton causes a downward shift in the supply curve from S to (S – subsidy), which results in an increase in the equilibrium quantity to 90 million tons per year and a decrease in the equilibrium price (paid by buyers) to $45 per ton. At the new equilibrium, farmers receive $75 per ton (the market price of $45, plus the $30 subsidy).

Recognizing that the (unsubsidized) supply curve represents the marginal cost and that the demand curve represents the marginal benefit, the marginal cost is greater than the marginal benefit at the new equilibrium with the subsidy. This leads to a deadweight loss from overproduction. The resources used to produce the additional 30 million tons of soybeans have a value in some other use that is greater than the value of these additional soybeans to consumers.

Figure 7: Soybean Price Subsidy

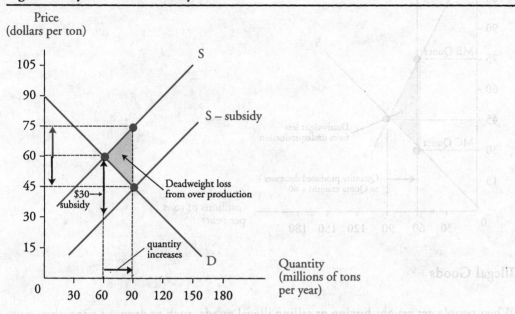

Price
(dollars per ton)

Production quotas are used to regulate markets by imposing an upper limit on the quantity of a good that may be produced over a specified time period. Quotas are often used by governments to regulate agricultural markets.

Continuing with our soybean example, let's suppose the government imposes a production quota on soybeans of 60 million tons per year. In Figure 8, we see that in the absence of a quota, soybean production is 90 million tons per year at a price of $45 per ton. With a 60 million ton quota, the equilibrium price rises to $75 per ton.

The reduction in the quantity of soybeans produced due to the quota leads to an inefficient allocation of resources and a deadweight loss to the economy. The quota not only increases the market price, but also lowers the marginal cost of producing the quota quantity. At the quota amount, marginal benefit (price) exceeds marginal cost. This explains why producers often seek the imposition of quotas.

Note that if a quota is greater than the equilibrium quantity of 90 million tons, nothing will change because farmers are already producing less than the maximum production allowed under the quota.

Figure 8: Soybean Production Quota

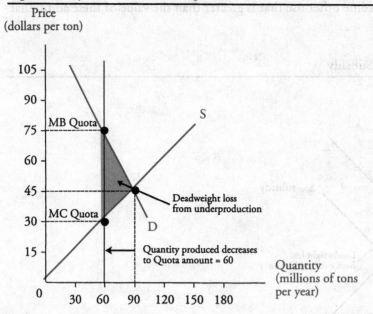

Illegal Goods

When people get caught buying or selling illegal goods, such as drugs or guns, they must pay penalties, including fines, imprisonment, or both. As the severity of the penalty or the likelihood of getting caught increases, the total costs of illegal trade increase. To see how the penalties from breaking the law affect the equilibrium quantity of an illegal good, consider the U.S. market for Cuban cigars illustrated in Figure 9. Here, the supply curve, S, represents the minimum prices that sellers would accept if Cuban cigars were legal, and the demand curve, D, represents the maximum prices that buyers would pay for Cuban cigars without any laws restricting their purchase. The equilibrium price and quantity under legal trade are at point L, where the equilibrium quantity is Q_L at a price of P_L. Because selling Cuban cigars is illegal in the United States, the compensation for the *expected penalty* for selling cigars, EP_S, is added to the sellers' minimum prices, shifting the supply curve in Figure 9 up to $S + EP_S$. If only sellers are penalized, the new equilibrium is represented by Point M.

In the United States, it is also illegal to purchase and possess Cuban cigars, so the cost of the expected penalties for buyers must be subtracted from the maximum price that buyers are willing to pay. This causes the demand curve to shift downward to $D - EP_D$. If only buyers were subject to the penalty, the Cuban cigar market would move from Point L to N.

When both buyers and sellers of illegal Cuban cigars must pay a penalty, the new equilibrium price and quantity are represented by Point O. As we have drawn it, the expected penalties for sellers and buyers are equal ($EP_S = EP_D$), so the new market price remains at the original market price, P_L, but the quantity purchased declines to Q^*. Effectively, buyers pay P_B, which is P_L plus an added cost equal to the value of the expected penalty for buying and possessing Cuban cigars, and sellers effectively receive P_S, which is P_L minus the amount to compensate for the expected penalty for selling

Cuban cigars. Note that buyers pay, and sellers receive, a cash price equal to P_L in this example.

The decrease in supply or demand for an illegal good increases as the value of the penalty increases. If the penalty is larger for the seller, the supply curve will shift by a greater amount than the demand curve, and the cash market price will rise above what it would have been if the good were not illegal, perhaps very significantly so. The opposite is true when penalties are higher for buyers.

Figure 9: Market for Illegal Cigars

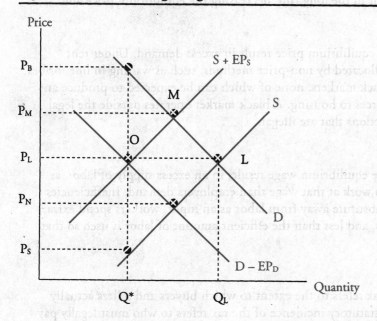

Good is Legal (Point L)

Cash price = P_L

Full cost to buyer = P_L

Net benefit to seller = P_L

Illegal to Sell (Point M)

Cash price = P_M

Full cost to buyer = P_M

Net benefit to seller = P_N

Illegal to Buy (Point N)

Cash price = P_N

Full cost to buyer = P_M

Net benefit to seller = P_N

Illegal to Buy or Sell (Point O)

Cash price = P_L

Full cost to buyer = P_B

Net benefit to seller = P_S

KEY CONCEPTS

LOS 15.a

Market equilibrium occurs at the price and quantity where the demand curve intersects the short-run supply curve.

Outside shocks that reduce short-run supply result in a higher equilibrium price and lower equilibrium quantity. If the market operates freely, the higher price will cause producers to increase output in the long run, decreasing the equilibrium price and increasing quantity.

Price ceilings set below the equilibrium price result in excess demand. Under rent control, housing must be allocated by non-price methods, such as waiting in line, bribes, decreases in quality, and black markets, none of which can be expected to produce an efficient allocation of resources to housing. A black market operates outside the legal system and refers to transactions that are illegal.

LOS 15.b

A minimum wage above the equilibrium wage results in an excess supply of labor, as more workers are willing to work at that wage than employers demand. Inefficiencies result because employers substitute away from labor as an input, workers spend extra time in job search activities, and less than the efficient amount of labor is used so that overall output declines.

LOS 15.c

The actual incidence of a tax refers to the extent to which buyers and sellers actually bear the cost of a tax. The statutory incidence of the tax refers to who must legally pay the tax.

Actual incidence of a tax is independent of who must legally pay the tax. The actual incidence falls more heavily on buyers when demand is less elastic than supply and more heavily on sellers when supply is less elastic than demand.

LOS 15.d

Subsidies increase production above the efficient quantity, resulting in deadweight losses from overproduction.

Production quotas that reduce output below the equilibrium level lead to deadweight losses from underproduction and prices higher than equilibrium prices.

The expected penalties for trading in illegal goods cause both demand and supply curves to shift to the left, decreasing the equilibrium quantities compared to what they would be if the goods were legal.

CONCEPT CHECKERS

1. A market that operates outside the legal system, having prices that exceed legally imposed price ceilings, is a:
   A. black market.
   B. subsidized market.
   C. quota controlled market.

2. Rent control is an example of a:
   A. quota.
   B. subsidy.
   C. price ceiling.

3. A minimum wage is an example of a:
   A. subsidy.
   B. price floor.
   C. price ceiling.

4. Quotas placed above the equilibrium quantity:
   A. increase marginal cost.
   B. result in overproduction.
   C. have no effect on output.

5. A subsidy:
   A. has no effect on output.
   B. leads to underproduction.
   C. shifts the supply curve down (to the right).

6. As a result of a production quota set below the equilibrium quantity:
   A. marginal benefit will exceed marginal cost.
   B. marginal cost will exceed marginal benefit.
   C. marginal benefit and marginal cost will decline.

7. Assume a good becomes illegal to buy or sell, and the expected penalty for selling the good is greater than that for buying the good. Relative to when the good was legal:
   A. price and quantity will rise.
   B. price and quantity will decline.
   C. price will rise and quantity will decline.

8. A price ceiling is only effective if it:
   A. is set above the equilibrium price.
   B. is set below the equilibrium price.
   C. has been in effect in over a relatively short time.

9. An example of a price floor is:
   A. rent control.
   B. a tax on ceramic tile.
   C. a minimum price for milk.

10.   The government imposes a tax on a good. The relative amounts of the tax that each economic actor in the market pays is called the:

    A. statutory tax.

    B. tax incidence.

    C. deadweight loss.

ANSWERS – CONCEPT CHECKERS

1. **A**   A black market is a market where trades of goods prohibited by law or trades at prices prohibited by law are made.

2. **C**   Rent controls are price ceilings and have the effect of reducing supply.

3. **B**   A minimum wage is a price floor and will likely increase unemployment.

4. **C**   A quota that is less than the equilibrium output quantity leads to a decrease in production and a deadweight loss from an inefficient allocation of resources. Quotas above the equilibrium quantity have no effect on output quantity.

5. **C**   A subsidy effectively shifts the supply curve to the right, which means a larger quantity is supplied at each price. The resulting new equilibrium will be at a quantity where marginal cost is greater than marginal benefit, so that there is an economic loss from production of more than the optimal amount of the subsidized good.

6. **A**   If output is forced to be below the equilibrium quantity, the marginal benefit will exceed the marginal cost and a deadweight loss comes about from underproduction.

7. **C**   If the expected penalty to sellers of illegal goods is greater than that to the buyers, the supply curve will shift up more than the demand curve will shift downward. The result is that price will rise and quantity will decline.

8. **B**   A price ceiling is only effective if it is lower than the equilibrium price without the ceiling. This leads to a shortage as consumers wish to purchase a quantity of the good at the ceiling price which is greater than the quantity supplied at that price.

9. **C**   A price floor is a minimum on the price that suppliers can charge. Such floors were once common in agricultural markets.

10. **B**   This is the definition of the incidence of a tax. It is determined by the shape of the supply and demand curves, not upon whom the tax is imposed legally (the statutory incidence of the tax).

The following is a review of the Economics principles designed to address the learning outcome statements set forth by CFA Institute®. This topic is also covered in:

ORGANIZING PRODUCTION

EXAM FOCUS

Make sure you can calculate economic profit, which requires that you identify relevant opportunity costs. Also, you should understand the different types of market competition and the issues surrounding the concentration measures of the degree of competition. The pros and cons of the different forms of business organization are another likely exam topic. You should also be able to differentiate between technological and economic efficiency. A basic understanding of the principal-agent problem will be sufficient here.

LOS 16.a: Explain the types of opportunity cost and their relation to economic profit, and calculate economic profit.

Opportunity cost is the return that a firm's resources could have earned elsewhere in its next most valuable use. Opportunity cost includes both explicit and implicit costs.

Explicit costs are observable, measurable expenses, such as the dollar cost of production inputs and the interest cost of renting (borrowing) capital.

Implicit costs are not explicitly observable and fall into two categories: (1) the opportunity cost to a firm of using its own capital, and (2) the opportunity cost of the time and financial resources of the firm's owners.

- The *implicit rental rate* is the term used to describe the opportunity cost to a firm for using its own capital. It represents what the firm could have earned if it had rented its capital (money and/or physical assets) to another firm. The implicit rental rate is the sum of (1) *economic depreciation*, which is the decrease in the value of a firm's assets over time, and (2) *foregone interest*.
- *Normal profit* is the opportunity cost of owners' **entrepreneurship** expertise. It represents what owners could have earned if they used their organizational, decision-making, and other entrepreneurial skills in another activity, such as running another business.

Economic profit considers both explicit and implicit costs. When the firm's revenues are just equal to its opportunity costs (i.e., explicit and implicit costs, including a normal profit), economic profits are zero. The computation of economic profit is illustrated in Figure 1.

Figure 1: Calculating Economic Profit for Patrick's Surfboard Company

Account		Amount
Total revenue		$340,000
Opportunity costs		
Fiberglass	$100,000	
Electricity	30,000	
Employee wages paid	55,000	
Interest paid on borrowed funds	5,000	
Total explicit costs		$190,000
Patrick's foregone wages	35,000	
Patrick's foregone interest	10,000	
Economic depreciation on buildings	5,000	
Normal profit	60,000	
Total implicit costs		$110,000
Total cost		$300,000
Economic profit		$40,000

 Professor's Note: Accounting profit only recognizes explicit costs, so it is greater than economic profit.

LOS 16.b: Discuss a firm's constraints and their impact on achievability of maximum profit.

Constrained profit maximization. Firms face three primary constraints as they endeavor to maximize profits: (1) technological, (2) information, and (3) market constraints.

Technology constraints. For our current purposes, technology may be defined simply as the means of producing a good or service. Technological developments are continuous. At any given point in time, a firm has the opportunity to increase output, and ultimately revenue, by employing additional technological resources. But to do so often means that the firm must incur additional costs. The additional profit from any increased output and revenue is limited by the cost of adopting new technology.

Information constraints. Profit maximization is constrained by the lack of information on which to base decisions. Many times, more information is available, but the cost of obtaining it may exceed its value (to increase firm profits). As with any productive resource, the firm will expend resources to acquire additional information only up to the point where the increase in total revenue from additional information is greater than the cost of the information.

Market constraints. Profits are also constrained by how much consumers are willing to pay for a firm's product or service and by the prices and marketing activities of its competitors. Resource markets also place constraints on profit maximization. The prices and availability of the resources that a firm uses and the willingness of people to invest in the firm present constraints on the firm's growth.

LOS 16.c: Differentiate between technological efficiency and economic efficiency and calculate economic efficiency of various firms under different scenarios.

Technological efficiency refers to using the least amount of specific inputs to produce a given output.

Economic efficiency refers to producing a given output at the lowest possible cost.

The difference between technological and economic efficiency is illustrated in the following example. Consider the four methods of producing a microwave oven illustrated in Figure 2.

Figure 2: Methods for Manufacturing 100 Microwave Ovens Per Day

| Method* | Input Quantities | |
	Capital (machine-day equivalent)	Labor (worker-days)
Robotic manufacturing (RM)	5,000	5
Assembly line manufacturing (ALM)	50	50
Workstation manufacturing (WSM)	50	500
Hand-crafted manufacturing (HCM)	5	5,000

*Method descriptions:

- RM requires one worker to monitor a completely robotic process.
- ALM requires the microwave assembly to be automatically moved from one work station to the next, where the worker at that station performs a specific, repetitive operation.
- WSM requires the workers to move from station to station to perform the same operation.
- HCM requires one worker to build an entire microwave oven using specialized tools.

An examination of the microwave oven manufacturing methods described in Figure 2 reveals that robotic manufacturing (RM) uses the most capital and least labor, whereas hand-crafted manufacturing (HCM) uses the most labor and least capital. Assembly line manufacturing (ALM) and workstation manufacturing (WSM) fall between these two extremes. WSM uses 50 units of capital and 500 units of labor to produce 100 ovens per day; ALM can also produce 100 ovens using 50 units of capital but requires only 50 units of labor. ALM is more *technologically efficient* than the WSM method because it uses absolutely less inputs to produce the same output.

Both the RM and HCM methods are technologically efficient because compared to ALM, RM uses less labor (but more capital), and HCM uses less capital (but more labor).

Economic efficiency is achieved when a given level of output is achieved at the least possible cost. Let's assume for our example that labor costs $75 per worker-day and capital costs $250 per machine-day. The costs of the four different methods are shown in Figure 3. ALM has the lowest cost per oven. Even though RM requires the least amount of labor, it requires more capital. On the other hand, while the HCM method requires the least amount of capital, it uses much more labor.

Recall that WSM is not technologically efficient. This fact ensures that WSM is not economically efficient either. WSM uses the same capital input ($12,500) as ALM but requires much more labor ($37,500 versus $3,750).

The total costs in Figure 3 will be different if the costs of labor and capital are different. Firms must routinely re-evaluate economic efficiency as the costs of inputs change.

Figure 3: Cost of Four Methods of Manufacturing 100 Microwave Ovens Per Day

Method	Capital Cost $250/unit	Labor Cost $75/unit	Total Cost	Cost Per Oven
RM	$1,250,000	$375	1,250,375	$12,503.75
ALM	12,500	3,750	16,250	162.50
WSM	12,500	37,500	50,000	500.00
HCM	1,250	375,000	376,250	3,762.50

LOS 16.d: Explain command systems and incentive systems to organize production, the principal-agent problem, and measures a firm uses to reduce the principal-agent problem.

Firms can organize production in two different ways: (1) command systems, and (2) incentive systems.

Command systems organize production according to a managerial chain of command. In a command system, managers spend much of their time processing information about the performance of the people who report to them, about what steps to take, and the best way to implement those steps. The U.S. military is an example of a command system; the President is at the top of the hierarchy. For a corporation using a command system of organizing production, the Chief Executive Officer is at the top of the system.

An **incentive system** is a means of organizing production whereby senior management creates a system of rewards intended to motivate workers to perform in such a way as to maximize profits. It is an effective system for organizing the production of a large sales force, where sales people may be paid a base salary that is relatively small and also rewarded for sales volume. CEOs are often subject to incentive systems, which provide them with compensation based on their firm's profit, sales, or stock price performance.

Command systems and incentive systems are often mixed within the same organization. Command systems are used when it is easy to monitor the performance of employees, as in the case of production workers. Incentive systems are usually most effective for organizing the production of employees whose activities are difficult or costly to monitor, like those of the firm's CEO and senior officers or outside sales people.

The **principal-agent problem** refers to the problems that arise when the incentives and motivations of managers and workers (agents) are not the same as the incentives and motivations of their firm's owners (principals). In many corporations, agents have their own goals, which may be different than those of the principals. For workers, there is often an incentive to shirk, which is to work below their normal level of productivity. At the managerial level, managers may work to maximize their own income and benefits rather than to maximize the value of the firm to its owners. The essence of the problem is that it is difficult or costly for the principals to monitor the actions of the agents.

Three methods are commonly used to reduce the principal-agent problem by better aligning the motivations of agents with those of principals: (1) ownership, (2) incentive pay, and (3) long-term contracts.

- When managers or workers have an *ownership* interest in the firm, it may motivate them to perform in a manner that maximizes the firm's profits or value. Ownership arrangements are commonly used with senior management, but less so for workers.
- *Incentive pay* is pay that is based on performance and is quite common in many industries. Incentive pay may be based on profits, sales, production quotas, or stock prices. Promotions may also be used as a form of incentive pay to align the interests of a firm's agents and principals.
- *Long-term contracts* for employment are often assigned to firms' CEOs to encourage them to develop strategies that will maximize profits over a relatively long period.

LOS 16.e: Describe the different types of business organization and the advantages and disadvantages of each.

Types of business organization. The three main forms of business organization are (1) proprietorships, (2) partnerships, and (3) corporations. Each form has its own advantages and disadvantages.

A **proprietorship** is a form of business organization with a single owner who has unlimited liability for the firm's debts and other legal obligations. Income flows through to the proprietor (owner) who pays taxes on it as personal income.

- *Advantages*: Easy to establish, simple decision-making process, and profits are only taxed once.
- *Disadvantages*: Decisions are not checked by a group consensus, the owner's entire wealth is exposed to risk, the business may cease to exist when the owner dies, and raising capital can be difficult and relatively expensive.

A **partnership** form of business organization involves two or more owners who both have unlimited liability for the debts and other legal obligations of the partnership. A partnership's taxable income is allocated (as personal income) to the partners based on their proportional ownership of the partnership.

- *Advantages*: Easy to establish, decision-making is diversified among partners, may survive even if a partner leaves or dies, and profits are only taxed once.
- *Disadvantages*: It can be difficult to achieve consensus decisions, owners' entire wealth is exposed to risk, and there may be a capital shortfall when a partner dies or leaves for other reasons. Since each partner may bring capital to the firm, capital is generally more readily available than for a proprietorship, but there are still significant limitations on the ability to raise large amounts of capital.

A **corporation** is owned by its stockholders, and their liability is legally limited to the amount of money they have invested in the firm. The firm is a legal entity that pays (corporate) income taxes. By far, corporations account for the largest share of revenue among the three types of business organizations.

- *Advantages*: Owners have limited liability, large amounts of relatively inexpensive capital are available, management expertise is not limited to that of the owners, a corporation's life is not limited to that of the owners, and long-term labor contracts can be used to reduce costs.
- *Disadvantages*: Relatively complex management structure may make the decision-making process slow and costly. Also, corporate earnings are taxed when earned and again when distributed to owners as dividends (i.e., double taxation).

> *Professor's Note: The most commonly cited advantages of the corporate form of business over proprietorships and partnerships is its unlimited access to relatively cheap capital and its limited liability to the owners. The biggest disadvantage of the corporate form over the other two forms is the double taxation of distributed profits.*

LOS 16.f: Calculate and interpret the four-firm concentration ratio and the Herfindahl-Hirschman Index, and discuss the limitations of concentration measures.

The concentration of a market refers to the distribution of firms' market shares. Markets with a few large firms are more concentrated than markets with many smaller firms. There are two primary measures of market concentration: (1) the four-firm concentration ratio, and (2) the Herfindahl-Hirschman Index.

The **four-firm concentration ratio** is the percentage of total industry sales made by the four largest firms in an industry. A highly competitive industry may have a four-firm concentration ratio near zero, while the ratio is 100% for a monopoly. A four-firm concentration ratio below 40% is considered an indication of a competitive market, and a four-firm ratio greater than 60% indicates an oligopoly.

The **Herfindahl-Hirschman Index** (HHI) is calculated by summing the squared percentage market shares of the 50 largest firms in an industry (or all of the firms in the industry if there are less than 50). The HHI is very low in a highly competitive industry and increases to 10,000 (= 100^2) for an industry with only one firm. An HHI between 1,000 and 1,800 is considered moderately competitive, while an HHI greater than 1,800 indicates a market that is not competitive.

 Professor's Note: Markets with varying degrees of competition (perfect competition, monopolistic competition, oligopoly, monopoly) are described in the next Study Session.

The usefulness of concentration measures as indicators of the degree of competition in a market is limited because of (1) problems with defining the geographical scope of the market; (2) barriers to entry and firm turnover in a market, which are not accounted for by these measures; and (3) weak relationships between a market and an industry.

The *geographical scope of the market* refers to the fact that products may be marketed in regional, local, or global markets. For example, concentration measures for newspapers in the global market are low, indicating a highly competitive market. But the concentration of newspapers in any given city is usually quite high, indicating relatively low competition at the local market level.

Barriers to entry and firm turnover in a market are not captured in concentration measures. While a small town may have few appliance stores, indicating a lack of competition, there is no barrier to opening a new appliance store, which increases the competitiveness of the market.

The *relationship between a market and an industry* is not always close, even though concentration measures assume that each firm fits neatly within one specific industry. There are three reasons why firms do not always fit neatly in a given industry. First, markets are often narrower than an industry. Companies may be in the same industry but sell specific products that do not compete with each other. Second, most large firms produce many different products, each facing different levels of competition. Concentration ratios, however, assume one market for the firm as a whole. Finally, firms may switch from one market to another in order to maximize profit. When firms can easily enter and exit a market, this *potential competition* increases the competitiveness of that market and limits firms' ability to generate economic profit.

LOS 16.g: Explain why firms are often more efficient than markets in coordinating economic activity.

Economic activity can be produced through market coordination or through firm coordination.

Market coordination is best described through an example. Consider the production of a heavyweight boxing match. The fight promoter secures an arena, a boxing ring, broadcast specialists, concession services, some boxers, a publicity agency, and a ticket agent. These are all market transactions. The promoter then sells tickets to the event through the ticket agent, along with broadcasting rights to a television network. So, the fight is produced through the coordination of markets.

Another example of market coordination is outsourcing. With outsourcing, a manufacturer of a product buys some or all of the product's components from other firms. The manufacturer then assembles all of the outsourced components to produce the final product. Outsourcing is a common practice in the automobile and personal computer industries.

Firm coordination occurs when firms can coordinate economic activity more efficiently than markets can. This is possible because firms can often achieve lower transaction costs, economies of scale, economies of scope, and economies of team production.

- *Transaction costs* refer to the costs associated with the negotiations that must take place when attempting to coordinate markets. Firms can often reduce transaction costs by reducing the number of individual transactions that must take place.
- *Economies of scale* exist when the average unit cost of producing a good decreases as output increases.
- *Economies of scope* occur when a firm can use its specialized resources to produce a range of goods and services. For example, a publisher hires editors, typists, reporters, marketing experts, and media distribution specialists and uses their skills across all of the firm's published products. This is less expensive to the publisher than it would be for an individual who attempted to hire these services individually in the markets.
- *Economies of team production* occur when a team of a firm's employees becomes highly efficient at a given task. It is usually less expensive for a firm with a well-honed team to produce a good or service than for an individual who has to hire the individual members of a team in the markets.

KEY CONCEPTS

LOS 16.a

Opportunity cost for a firm is the value of the resources it owns in their next-highest-valued productive use.

Explicit costs are measurable expenses. Implicit costs include the implicit rental rate (the opportunity cost to a firm from the use of its own capital assets) and normal profit (the opportunity cost associated with the use of the owners' time, resources, and entrepreneurship expertise).

Economic profit is total revenue minus both explicit and implicit costs.

LOS 16.b

The three primary constraints on profit maximization are the level of technology (additional profit from increased output is limited by the cost of adopting new technology), information (the cost of obtaining additional information may exceed its value), and the characteristics of the markets for the company's output and of the markets for the resources the company employs.

LOS 16.c

A production method is technologically efficient if no other method can produce the same output with less of one input and no more of any other input. A production method is economically efficient if output is produced at a lower cost than by any other method.

LOS 16.d

Command systems organize production according to a chain of command. Incentive systems organize production through a system of rewards for results.

The principal-agent problem exists because agents (managers and workers) do not have the same motives and incentives as the firm's principals (owners).

Ownership interests, incentive pay, and long-term employment contracts are used to reduce the effects of the principal-agent problem.

LOS 16.e

A proprietorship is a business with a single owner. It is easy to start, has a simple decision process, and its profits are only taxed once as personal income; however, there are no decision reviews, the owner has unlimited liability, the business may cease to exist if its proprietor dies, and its ability to raise capital is limited to debt incurred by the proprietor.

A partnership is a business with two or more owners. It is easy to start, its decisions are reviewed by partners, it can survive if a partner leaves or dies, and its taxable income is allocated among the partners; however, it may be difficult to reach consensus decisions, each partner has unlimited liability, there may be a capital shortfall if a partner leaves, and access to capital is limited compared to a corporate structure.

A corporation is a legal entity owned by its stockholders who each have liability limited to the capital they have contributed to the firm. A corporation can raise large amounts of capital, has managerial expertise that is not limited to that of the owners, and has an unlimited life; however, corporations are burdened by complex management structures and double taxation of profits that are distributed to shareholders.

LOS 16.f

Market concentration measures indicate the degree of competition.

* The four-firm concentration ratio is the sum of the percentage market shares of the four largest firms in an industry (below 40% is competitive).
* The Herfindahl-Hirschman Index is the sum of the squared percentage market shares of the 50 largest firms in an industry (greater than 1,800 is not competitive).

The usefulness of concentration measures can be limited because: (1) there are problems with defining the geographical scope of the market, (2) these measures do not account for barriers to entry and firm turnover, and (3) there can be a weak relationship between markets and the definition of industries for which the measures are calculated.

LOS 16.g

Companies can often coordinate economic activity more efficiently than markets by reducing transaction costs and by achieving economies of scale (greater production of a single product), scope (resources used across several products), and team production.

CONCEPT CHECKERS

1. Economic profits are zero if:
   A. implicit costs equal explicit costs.
   B. economic depreciation equals zero.
   C. total revenue equals the sum of all opportunity costs.

2. Assume that a firm had total revenue of $50 million and used $30 million in labor and materials to generate that revenue. Other costs included $100,000 in foregone interest and economic depreciation of $20,000. Normal profit is $65,000. Using this information, calculate the economic profit to the firm.
   A. $19,815,000.
   B. $19,856,000.
   C. $20,000,000.

3. Which of the following statements regarding technological and economic efficiency is *most accurate*?
   A. Whenever an activity is technologically efficient, it must be economically efficient.
   B. For a given output, a technologically efficient method uses the least amount of inputs and an economically efficient method has lowest possible cost.
   C. For a given output, a technologically efficient method uses the least amount of labor and an economically efficient method uses the least amount of capital.

4. Consider two markets: one has a Herfindahl-Hirschman Index (HHI) of 500, while the other has a four-firm ratio concentration ratio equal to 2%. Which of the following statements *most accurately* describes these two markets?
   A. Both markets are highly competitive.
   B. The market with the HHI equal to 500 is very competitive, while the other market has a low degree of competition.
   C. The market with the HHI equal to 500 has a low degree of competition, while the other market is highly competitive.

5. The implied rental rate includes:
   A. foregone interest and normal profit.
   B. economic depreciation and normal profit.
   C. economic depreciation and foregone interest.

6. An industry with a Herfindahl-Hirschman Index (HHI) of 2,800 and a four-firm concentration ratio of 75% is *most likely* competing in which type of market?
   A. Oligopoly.
   B. Monopoly.
   C. Competitive.

7. Which of the following would *least likely* be used to reduce the principal-agent problem in corporations?
   A. Use of a company jet.
   B. An incentive-pay system.
   C. Long-term employment contracts.

8. Which of the following statements *least accurately* describes why companies can sometimes coordinate economic activity more efficiently than markets? Companies can achieve economies of:
   A. scale.
   B. scope.
   C. cost.

9. Consider two manufacturing processes that can be used to produce the same quantity of a given product. Process A uses 10 units of labor and 50 units of physical capital. Process B uses 10 units of labor and 500 units of capital. Which of the following *most accurately* describes these processes?
   A. Process A is economically efficient and technologically efficient.
   B. Process B is technologically inefficient and economically efficient.
   C. Process A is technologically efficient and either process may be economically efficient.

ANSWERS – CONCEPT CHECKERS

1. **C** Economic profit considers both explicit and implicit opportunity costs. When total revenues are just equal to opportunity costs (explicit and implicit, including normal profit), economic profits are zero.

2. **A** Economic profit = total revenue – opportunity costs = total revenue – (explicit + implicit costs). In this case, the labor and material cost of $30 million is the explicit cost. Implicit costs include the $100,000 in foregone interest, economic depreciation of $20,000, and normal profit of $65,000. So, total implicit costs equal $100,000 + $20,000 + $65,000 = $185,000. Thus, economic profit is $50,000,000 – $30,000,000 – $185,000 = $19,815,000.

3. **B** Technological efficiency is achieved by using the least amount of inputs to produce a given output. Economic efficiency is achieved by producing a given output at the lowest possible cost.

4. **A** An HHI of 500 is low, indicating a high degree of competition. A four-firm concentration ratio of 2% indicates a high level of competition. The higher (lower) the concentration measure, the lower (greater) the degree of competition.

5. **C** The implied rental rate includes economic depreciation and foregone interest. When discussing economic profit, economic depreciation is the decrease in the value of an asset while that asset is being used to produce a product.

6. **A** A monopoly market has a Herfindahl-Hirschman Index of 10,000 and a four-firm concentration ratio of 100%. An HHI index greater than 1,800 indicates an uncompetitive market, and a four-firm concentration ratio greater than 60% indicates an oligopoly market. Therefore, the firms in the industry described are most likely in an oligopoly market.

7. **A** A company jet could be a symptom of a principal-agent problem and does not address a divergence of incentives. The other choices are common methods to reduce the principal-agent problem.

8. **C** Companies can often coordinate economic activity more efficiently than markets because companies can reduce the costs of market transactions, and they can achieve economies of scale, scope, and team production. Economies of cost is a made-up term.

9. **A** Process A is technologically efficient because for the same 10 units of labor, it can produce the given output with less capital. For any prices of capital and labor, Process A must have a lower cost, so it is also the economically efficient process.

OUTPUT AND COSTS

EXAM FOCUS

This review is primarily focused on the relationship between short-run costs and output. You should know how total, marginal, and average product relate to the components of total cost. Be able to describe diminishing returns to labor and capital, and understand the long-run conditions that lead to economies of scale.

LOS 17.a: Differentiate between short-run and long-run decision time frames.

The **short run** is defined as a time period for which quantities of some resources are fixed. A firm has chosen its production methods and, if it is a manufacturer, the machinery it will use to produce its products. In the **long run**, a firm can adjust its input quantities, production methods, and plant size.

So the technology of production is fixed in the short run and is a constraint on a firm's ability to increase production. Typically, economists treat labor and raw materials as variable in the short run, holding plant size, capital equipment, and technology constant. All of these factors become variable in the long run.

Short-run decisions, such as adjusting labor and raw materials inputs, are easier to reverse than long-run decisions, such as investing in new technology or capital assets. Capital that has been spent on a long-run project is typically a **sunk cost** which (as we will see in the Study Session on Corporate Finance) managers should not consider when making investment decisions.

LOS 17.b: Describe and explain the relations among total product of labor, marginal product of labor, and average product of labor, and describe increasing and decreasing marginal returns.

In what follows, we will examine output in the short run, allowing only the quantity of labor employed to vary.

The table in Figure 1 contains output information for a hypothetical maker of shirts, Sam's Shirts. The first column of the table lists different quantities of workers per day that can be employed. The second column lists the total number of shirts per day that Sam's can produce with different numbers of workers, holding plant and equipment constant. This total output of shirts is called the **total product**. The third column has the number of additional shirts per day from adding each successive worker. This is the **marginal product** of labor, the additional output from adding one more unit (in this case one worker-day) of labor. The fourth column lists the average number of shirts per worker that are produced for each quantity of workers. This is the **average product** of labor. Note that the units of total, marginal, and average product are units of the good produced per unit of the input under consideration, in this case, shirts per worker day.

Figure 1: Short-Run Output as a Function of Labor Employed

Workers	Total Product	Marginal Product	Average Product
1	8	8	8
2	20	12	10
3	26	6	8.7
4	30	4	7.5
5	32	2	6.4
6	33	1	5.5

Panel (a) and Panel (b) of Figure 2 show the total product curve and marginal product curve, respectively, for Sam's Shirts. The total and marginal product curves in Figure 2 have been smoothed to account for fractional worker days. The total product curve can be viewed as a *production possibilities frontier*. The area above the curve represents output that cannot be produced by the given number of workers. The area below the curve represents technologically inefficient production because more labor than necessary is being used to produce each level of output.

Note that the marginal product curve shown in Panel (b) of Figure 2 initially increases, reaches a peak, and then begins to decline. This behavior is typical. The marginal product curve for an input typically shows increasing marginal returns initially, and decreasing marginal returns at some point. **Decreasing marginal returns** describes a situation where the marginal product of an input decreases as additional units of that input are employed.

Figure 2: Total Product and Marginal Product

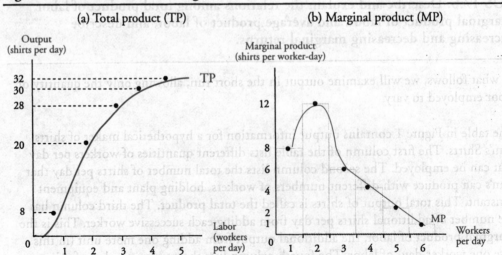

©2010 Kaplan, Inc.

Figure 3 shows the relation between the average product curve for Sam's Shirts and the marginal product curve. Note in Figure 3 that average product is at its maximum at the point where the marginal product curve intersects it from above. For Sam's Shirts, this intersection occurs between two and three workers per day. Note that for the second worker, MP is greater than AP, but with three workers, MP is less than AP. This relationship is not unique to Sam's Shirts. Typically, marginal product exceeds average product up to some input quantity where they are equal. Beyond that point, marginal product is less than average product.

Figure 3: Average Product and Marginal Product of Labor

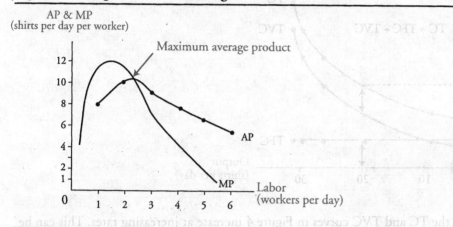

LOS 17.c: Distinguish among total cost (including both fixed cost and variable cost), marginal cost, and average cost, and explain the relations among the various cost curves.

To increase output in the short run, firms must use more labor, which increases cost. The relationship between output and cost may be explained in terms of three cost concepts: (1) total cost, (2) marginal cost, and (3) average cost.

Total cost (TC) is the sum of all costs associated with the generation of output. Total cost is made up of total *fixed* cost and total *variable* cost.

Total fixed cost (TFC) is the cost of fixed inputs, such as property, plant, and equipment, plus *normal profit* (i.e., the value of the entrepreneurial ability of the firm's owners or managers). Total fixed cost is independent of the level of the firm's output in the short run.

Total variable cost (TVC) is the cost of all variable production inputs. Total variable cost increases as output increases. The single biggest variable cost for most firms is the cost of labor (and raw materials for manufacturing firms).

total cost = total fixed cost + total variable cost

Figure 4 illustrates the components of total cost for Sam's Shirts at different output levels. We will assume that Sam's fixed cost is $20 per day to rent one sewing machine. This amount will not change regardless of the quantity of shirts produced. So, the TFC curve is a horizontal line at $20 per day.

For simplicity, assume that labor is the only variable cost, and that Sam pays his workers $20 per day. So total variable cost will increase by $20 as each additional worker is required to increase output. Notice in Figure 4 that the vertical distance between the TVC and the TC curves is total fixed cost. It is also important to note that both TVC and TC are increasing. This is because TVC increases as output increases.

Figure 4: Total Cost Curves

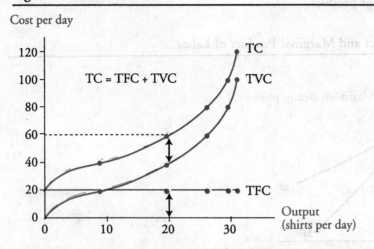

Notice that the TC and TVC curves in Figure 4 increase at increasing rates. This can be explained through a discussion of the concept of marginal cost.

Marginal cost, MC, is the increase in total cost for one additional unit of output. Since the addition of each worker results in multiple additional shirts, we divide the change in total cost by the increase in output to get the marginal cost amounts in Figure 5. That is:

$$\text{marginal cost} = \frac{\text{change in total cost}}{\text{change in output}}, \text{ or } MC = \frac{\Delta TC}{\Delta Q}$$

The relationships among TFC, TVC, MC, AFC, AVC, and ATC are shown for increasing amounts of labor and output in Figure 5.

Figure 5: Total, Marginal, and Average Costs for Sam's Shirts

Output (shirts)	Labor (workers/day)	TFC ($/day)	TVC	TC	MC ($/additional shirt)	AFC ($/shirt)	AVC	ATC
0	0	20	0	20				
					-----2.50-----			
8	1	20	20	40		2.50	2.50	5.00
					----1.67-----			
20	2	20	40	60		1.00	2.00	3.00
					-----3.33-----			
26	3	20	60	80		0.77	2.31	3.08
					-----5.00-----			
30	4	20	80	100		0.67	2.67	3.33
					----10.00----			
32	5	20	100	120		0.63	3.13	3.75

TFC = Total fixed cost	cost of fixed inputs; independent of output	-----5.00-----
TVC = Total variable cost	cost of variable inputs; changes with output	
TC = Total cost		-----10.00-----
MC = Marginal cost	change in total cost for one unit increase in output	$MC = \Delta TC / \Delta Q$
AFC = Average fixed cost		$AFC = TFC / Q$
AVC = Average variable cost		$AVC = TVC / Q$
ATC = Average total cost		$ATC = AFC + AVC$

Example: Marginal cost

Using the information for Sam's Shirts presented in Figure 5, calculate the marginal cost per shirt when output increases from 8 to 20 shirts per day.

Answer:

In Figure 5, we see that the change in TC when output increases from eight to 20 shirts is $60 – $40 = $20. Since the change in output is 20 – 8 = 12 shirts, the marginal cost can be calculated as:

MC = $20 / 12 shirts = $1.67 per shirt

Average cost is the average cost per unit of output at a given level of output. Since there are three types of costs, there are three corresponding average costs. These are:

- Average fixed cost (AFC), total fixed cost per unit of output.
- Average variable cost (AVC), total variable cost per unit of output.
- Average total cost (ATC), total cost per unit of output.

The individual average costs are calculated by dividing the total costs at a given level of output, Q, by that level of output. Mathematically, we have:

$$\frac{TC}{Q} = \frac{TFC}{Q} + \frac{TVC}{Q}, \text{ or } ATC = AFC + AVC$$

Average costs at the various output levels for Sam's have been calculated and tabulated in Figure 5. The marginal cost (MC) and average cost (ATC, AVC, and AFC) curves for Sam's Shirts are shown in Figure 6.

Figure 6: Average and Marginal Costs

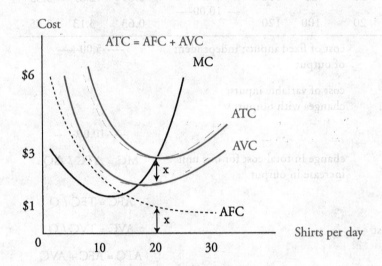

Important relationships among the marginal and average cost curves in Figure 6 are:

- *AFC slopes downward.* This is because fixed costs are constant but are distributed over a larger and larger number of products as output quantity increases.
- *The vertical distance between the ATC and AVC curves is equal to AFC.* This is indicated by the arrows marked "x" at an output of 20 shirts per day.
- *MC declines initially, then increases.* At low output quantities, efficiencies are realized from the specialization of labor. However, as more and more labor is added, marginal cost increases. This is due to *diminishing returns*, which means that at some point, each added worker contributes less to total output than the previously added worker.
- *MC intersects AVC and ATC at their minimum points.* The intersection comes from below, which implies that when MC is less than ATC or AVC, respectively, ATC or AVC are decreasing. This also implies that when MC exceeds ATC or AVC, respectively, ATC or AVC are increasing.
- *ATC and AVC are U-shaped.* AVC decreases initially, but as output increases, the effect of diminishing returns sets in and AVC eventually slopes upward, giving the curve its U-shape. However, since fixed costs are spread out over a larger and larger quantity of output, AFC decreases as output increases, and eventually flattens out. ATC gets its U-shape because as output increases we are adding a curve that goes from downward sloping to flat (AFC) to a U-shaped curve (AVC), which results in a U-shaped ATC curve. Remember, ATC = AVC + AFC.

The relationship between product curves and cost curves is illustrated in Figure 7, where average and marginal product curves for a firm are presented in Panel (a), and marginal and average cost curves are presented in Panel (b). Figure 7 illustrates the following important links between a firm's product curves (technology) and its cost curves.

- Over the initial increase in labor from zero to L_1 in Panel (a), MP and AP increase and MP reaches its maximum. Over the corresponding output range in Panel (b), MC and AVC decrease to output quantity Q_1 where MC is at a minimum. Note that L_1 is the labor required to produce Q_1.
- As labor increases from L_1 to L_2 and output increases from Q_1 to Q_2, AP continues to increase to a maximum at L_2, and AVC continues to fall to its minimum at Q_2. Over this same production range, MP is declining and MC is rising.
- As labor increases beyond L_2 and output increases beyond Q_2, MP and AP both decrease, and MC and AVC both increase.

Figure 7: Product and Cost Curves

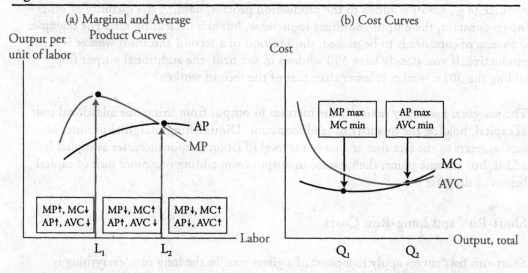

LOS 17.d: Explain the firm's production function, its properties of diminishing returns and diminishing marginal product of capital, the relation between short-run and long-run costs, and how economies and diseconomies of scale affect long-run costs.

A firm's **production function** is the relationship between its inputs of capital and labor and the quantity of output it can produce. Figure 8 shows a possible production function for Sam's Shirts. Notice that as the firm adds more units of labor or capital, the resulting increase in output reaches a maximum and then starts to get smaller. This illustrates the fact that productive inputs exhibit **diminishing returns**.

Figure 8: Production Function for Sam's Shirts

Labor (hours/day)	Capital (sewing machines used)					
	1	2	3	4	5	6
40	6	9	12	14	16	17
48	8	12	16	20	23	25
56	11	15	20	24	27	30
64	13	18	23	27	31	34
80	15	20	25	30	34	37
88	16	21	27	32	36	39

The **law of diminishing returns** states that at some point, as more and more of one resource (e.g., labor) is added to the production process, holding the quantity of other inputs constant, the output continues to increase, but at a decreasing rate. For example, if an acre of corn needs to be picked, the addition of a second and third worker is highly productive. If you already have 300 workers in the field, the additional output from adding the 301st worker is lower than that of the second worker.

The *marginal product of capital* is the increase in output from using one additional unit of capital, holding the quantity of labor constant. **Diminishing marginal product of capital** refers to the fact that at a constant level of labor, output increases as capital is added, but at some point, the increase in output from adding one more unit of capital begins to decrease.

Short-Run and Long-Run Costs

Short-run cost curves apply to a plant of a given size. In the long run, everything is variable, including technology, plant size, and equipment. Long-run cost curves are known as *planning curves*. There is often a trade-off between the size of the firm and unit costs in the long run.

Three reasons unit cost may decline as output or plant size increase are:

1. Savings due to mass production.
2. Specialization of labor and machinery.
3. Experience.

The downward sloping segment of the long-run average total cost curve presented in Figure 9 indicates that **economies of scale** are present. In this range increasing the scale (size) of the firm results in lower average unit costs. The upward sloping segment of this long-run average total cost curve indicates that **diseconomies of scale** are present when average unit costs rise as the scale of the business increases. The flat portion of the long-run average total costs curve in Figure 9 represents *constant returns to scale*. As shown, the firm's **minimum efficient scale** (the firm size that will minimize average unit costs) is one which will produce Q* units of output.

Figure 9: Long-Run Average Total Cost

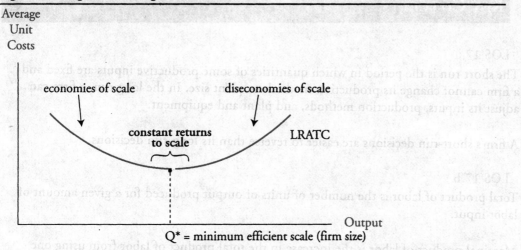

Diseconomies of scale may result as the increasing bureaucracy of larger firms leads to inefficiency, as well as from problems of motivating a larger workforce, greater barriers to innovation and entrepreneurial activity, and increased principal-agent problems.

KEY CONCEPTS

LOS 17.a

The short run is the period in which quantities of some productive inputs are fixed and a firm cannot change its production methods or plant size. In the long run, a firm can adjust its inputs, production methods, and plant and equipment.

A firm's short-run decisions are easier to reverse than its long-run decisions.

LOS 17.b

Total product of labor is the number of units of output produced for a given amount of labor input.

Marginal product of labor is the increase in the total product of labor from using one additional unit of labor, holding the quantities of other inputs fixed.

Average product of labor is total product of labor divided by the units of labor used.

Marginal product increases at first as more labor is added to a fixed amount of capital assets (increasing marginal returns) but eventually decreases as more labor is added (diminishing marginal returns). The marginal product of labor curve intersects the average product of labor curve at its maximum.

LOS 17.c

Total cost is the sum of total fixed cost (e.g., plant and equipment), which does not vary with output, and total variable cost (e.g., labor, raw materials), which increases as output is increased.

Marginal cost is the increase in total cost for a one unit increase in output.

Average fixed cost (AFC) is fixed cost per unit of output. Average variable cost (AVC) is variable cost per unit of output. Average total cost (ATC) is total cost per unit of output. ATC = AFC + AVC.

AFC slopes downward in the short run because fixed costs are constant, but are averaged over an increasing quantity of output. The vertical distance between the ATC and AVC curves is equal to AFC.

The marginal cost curve intersects the AVC and ATC curves from below at their minimum points.

The AVC curve is U-shaped, declining at first due to efficiency gains, but eventually increasing due to diminishing returns. The ATC curve is U-shaped because it is the sum of the decreasing-to-flat AFC curve and the U-shaped AVC curve.

LOS 17.d

A production function illustrates the relationship between a firm's labor and capital inputs and its quantity of output.

The law of diminishing returns states that, at some point, using more of a variable input (holding other input quantities constant) increases output at a decreasing rate.

Diminishing marginal product of capital means that for a constant quantity of labor, output increases at a decreasing rate as more capital is employed.

Short-run cost curves are specific to a given plant size. Long-run average cost curves show minimum average unit costs based on the optimal plant size (scale of operations) for each level of output.

Economies of scale are present when unit costs fall as plant size increases. Diseconomies of scale are present when costs rise as plant size increases, often arising from the bureaucratic inefficiencies that occur with larger firms.

CONCEPT CHECKERS

1. Which of the following *most accurately* describes the relationship between marginal product (MP) and average product (AP) of labor in the short run? As the quantity of output increases:
    A. AP is always less than MP.
    B. initially, AP < MP, then AP = MP, then AP > MP.
    C. initially, AP > MP, then AP = MP, then AP < MP.

2. When marginal product is at a maximum:
    A. marginal cost is at a minimum.
    B. average product is at a minimum.
    C. average variable cost is at a minimum.

3. When average product is at a maximum:
    A. marginal cost is at a minimum.
    B. marginal product is at a minimum.
    C. average variable cost is at a minimum.

4. As a result of increasing labor from 100 to 110 workers, output increased from 1,250 to 1,550 units per day. The marginal product of an additional worker is *closest* to:
    A. 1.55 units per day.
    B. 30 units per day.
    C. 300 units per day.

5. If both average product (AP) and marginal product (MP) are equal to 8 when 10 workers are employed, what can we *most likely* conclude about AP and MP when 15 workers are employed?
    A. AP = MP = 5.
    B. AP = 4 and MP = 6.
    C. AP = 7 and MP = 5.

6. Which of the following *most accurately* describes the shapes of the average variable cost (AVC) curve and average total cost (ATC) curve?
    A. The AVC curve and the ATC curve are both U-shaped.
    B. The AVC curve is U-shaped; the ATC curve declines initially then flattens.
    C. The AVC curve declines initially then flattens; the ATC curve is U-shaped.

7. The vertical distance between the average total cost (ATC) curve and average variable cost (AVC) curve:
    A. increases as output increases.
    B. decreases as output increases.
    C. remains constant as output increases.

8. Which of the following *most accurately* describes the shape of the average fixed cost curve?
    A. It becomes relatively flat at large output levels.
    B. It is always below the average variable cost curve.
    C. It intersects the marginal cost curve at its minimum.

©2010 Kaplan, Inc.

9. Economies of scale:
    A. are dependent on short-run average costs.
    B. occur when average unit costs fall with larger firm size.
    C. occur when the long-run average cost curve is sloping upward.

10. For a fixed level of capital, output increases as the quantity of labor increases, but at a decreasing rate. This phenomenon is *most accurately* described by the law of diminishing:
    A. returns to labor.
    B. returns to capital.
    C. returns to technology.

ANSWERS – CONCEPT CHECKERS

1. **B**   MP intersects the AP maximum from above. MP is initially greater than AP, and then MP and AP intersect. Beyond this intersection, MP is less than AP. (Hint: draw the curves.)

2. **A**   Marginal product is at a maximum when marginal cost is at a minimum. At the corresponding labor and output levels, average variable cost is decreasing and average product is increasing.

3. **C**   When average product is at a maximum, average variable cost is at a minimum. At the corresponding labor and output level, marginal product is decreasing and marginal cost is increasing.

4. **B**   Marginal product is the change in output divided by the change in input (labor). Since output changed by 300 units and labor changed by 10 workers, the marginal product is 300 / 10 = 30 units per day.

5. **C**   For most production processes, as the quantity of labor increases, marginal product is initially greater than average product. Then at some level of labor input, the two curves intersect. Beyond this intersection, marginal product is less than average product. So, beyond AP = MP = 8, MP must be less than AP.

6. **A**   The AVC curve is U-shaped, declining at first due to efficiency, but eventually increasing due to diminishing returns. The AFC curve decreases as output increases, and eventually flattens out. The ATC is U-shaped because it is the sum of the decreasing-to-flat AFC curve plus the U-shaped AVC curve. ATC = AFC + AVC.

7. **B**   The vertical distance between the average total cost curve and average variable cost curve is average fixed cost, which decreases as output increases because more output is averaged over the same cost.

8. **A**   Average fixed cost initially declines rapidly, but as output increases it flattens out, because fixed cost is being averaged over more and more units of output.

9. **B**   Economies of scale occur when the percentage increase in output is greater than the percentage increase in cost of all inputs. They occur when the long-run average cost curve slopes downward.

10. **A**   The law of diminishing returns states that at some point, as more and more of a resource (e.g., labor) is devoted to a production process, holding the quantity of other inputs constant, the output increases, but at a decreasing rate.

The following is a review of the Economics principles designed to address the learning outcome statements set forth by CFA Institute®. This topic is also covered in:

PERFECT COMPETITION

Study Session 5

EXAM FOCUS

You should be able to explain what a price-taker market is and how price and output are determined in the short run and the long run. Pay special attention to the relationship between marginal cost, marginal revenue, price, and output for a perfectly competitive firm. Know how the concept of economic profit applies to perfect competition. Finally, you should be able to explain the adjustments that take place in response to changes in industry demand. A good understanding of the case of perfect competition is important because this is the model of economically efficient markets to which we will compare other market structures in the reviews that follow.

LOS 18.a: Describe the characteristics of perfect competition, explain why firms in a perfectly competitive market are price takers, and differentiate between market and firm demand curves.

Price takers are firms that face horizontal (perfectly elastic) demand curves. They can sell all of their output at the prevailing market price, but if they set their output price higher than the market price, they would sell nothing. They are price takers because they take the market price as given and do not have to devote any resources to discovering the best price at which to sell their product. A "price-taker market" is equivalent to a perfectly competitive market.

Perfect competition assumes the following:

- All the firms in the market produce identical products.
- There is a large number of independent firms.
- Each seller is small relative to the size of the total market.
- There are no barriers to entry or exit.

Producer firms in perfect competition have no influence over market price. Market supply and demand determine price. As illustrated in Figure 1, the *individual firm's* demand schedule is *perfectly elastic* (horizontal).

Figure 1: Price-Taker Demand

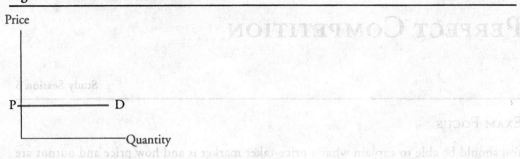

In a perfectly competitive market, a firm will continue to expand production until marginal revenue (MR) equals marginal cost (MC). Marginal revenue is the increase in total revenue from selling one more unit of a good or service. For a price taker, marginal revenue is simply the price because all additional units are assumed to be sold at the same (market) price. In *pure competition*, a firm's marginal revenue is equal to the market price, and a firm's MR curve, presented in Figure 2, is identical to its demand curve. A profit maximizing firm will produce the quantity, Q*, when MC = MR.

Figure 2: Profit Maximizing Output For A Price Taker

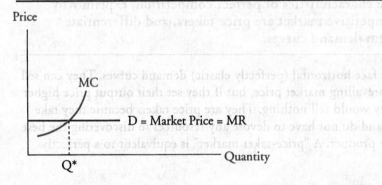

LOS 18.b: Determine the profit maximizing (loss minimizing) output for a perfectly competitive firm, and explain marginal cost, marginal revenue, and economic profit and loss.

All firms maximize (economic) profit by producing and selling the quantity for which marginal revenue equals marginal cost. For a price taker in a perfectly competitive market, this is the same as producing and selling the output for which marginal revenue equals (market) price. Economic profit equals total revenues less the opportunity cost of production, which includes the cost of a normal return to all factors of production, including invested capital.

Figure 3(a) illustrates that in the *short run*, economic profit is maximized when marginal revenue = marginal cost = price, or MR = MC = P. As shown in Figure 3(b), profit maximization also occurs when total revenue exceeds total cost by the maximum amount.

An *economic loss* occurs on any units for which marginal revenue is less than marginal cost. At any output above the quantity where MR = MC, the firm will be generating losses on its marginal production and will maximize profits by reducing output to where MR = MC.

Figure 3: Short-Run Profit Maximization

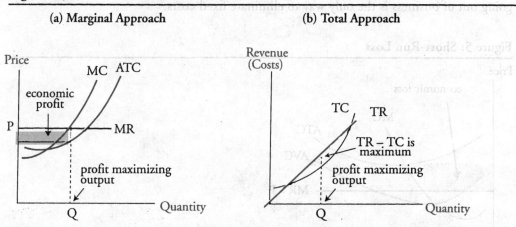

In a perfectly competitive market, a firm will not earn economic profits for any significant period of time. The assumption is that new firms (with average and marginal cost curves identical to those of existing firms) will enter the industry to earn profits, increasing market supply and eventually reducing market price so that it just equals a firm's average total cost (ATC). In equilibrium, each firm is producing the quantity for which P = MR = MC = ATC, so that no firm earns economic profits and each firm is producing the quantity for which ATC is a minimum (the quantity for which ATC = MC). This is illustrated in Figure 4.

Figure 4: Equilibrium in a Perfectly Competitive Market

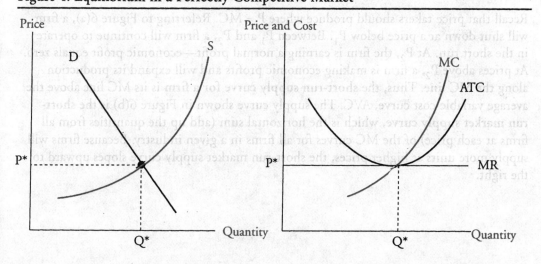

Figure 5 illustrates that firms will experience economic losses when price is below average total cost (P < ATC). In this case, the firm must decide whether to continue operating. A firm will minimize its losses in the short run by continuing to operate when P < ATC but P > AVC. As long as the firm is covering its variable costs and some of its fixed costs, its loss will be less than its fixed (in the short run) costs. If the firm is only just covering its variable costs (P = AVC), the firm is operating at its **shutdown point**. If the firm is not covering its variable costs (P < AVC) by continuing to operate, its losses will be greater than its fixed costs. In this case, the firm will shut down (zero output) and lay off its workers. This will limit its losses to its fixed costs (e.g., its building lease and debt payments). If the firm does not believe price will ever exceed ATC in the future, going out of business is the only way to eliminate fixed costs.

Figure 5: Short-Run Loss

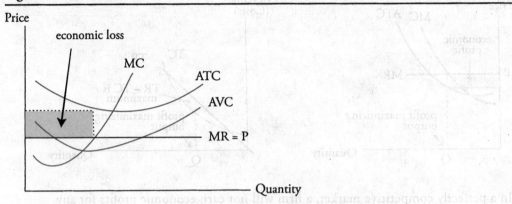

The *long-run equilibrium output* level for perfectly competitive firms is where MR = MC = ATC, which is where ATC is at a minimum. At this output, economic profit is zero and only a normal return is realized.

LOS 18.c: Describe a perfectly competitive firm's short-run supply curve and explain the impact of changes in demand, entry and exit of firms, and changes in plant size on the long-run equilibrium.

Recall that price takers should produce where P = MC. Referring to Figure 6(a), a firm will shut down at a price below P_1. Between P_1 and P_2, a firm will continue to operate in the short run. At P_2, the firm is earning a normal profit—economic profit equals zero. At prices above P_2, a firm is making economic profits and will expand its production along the MC line. Thus, the **short-run supply curve for a firm** is its MC line above the average variable cost curve, AVC. The supply curve shown in Figure 6(b) is the **short-run market supply curve**, which is the horizontal sum (add up the quantities from all firms at each price) of the MC curves for all firms in a given industry. Because firms will supply more units at higher prices, the short-run market supply curve slopes upward to the right.

Figure 6: Short-Run Supply Curves

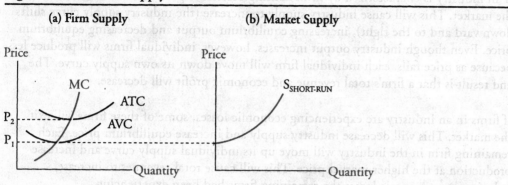

Changes in Demand, Entry and Exit, and Changes in Plant Size

In the short run, an increase in market demand (a shift of the market demand curve to the right) will increase both equilibrium price and quantity, while a decrease in market demand will reduce both equilibrium price and quantity. The change in equilibrium price will change the (horizontal) demand curve faced by each individual firm and the profit-maximizing output of a firm. These effects for an increase in demand are illustrated in Figure 7. An increase in market demand from D_1 to D_2 increases the short-run equilibrium price from P_1 to P_2 and equilibrium output from Q_1 to Q_2. In Figure 7(b), we see the short-run effect of the increased market price on the output of an individual firm. The higher price leads to a greater profit-maximizing output, $Q_{2\ Firm}$. At the higher output level, a firm will earn an economic profit in the short run. In response to the increase in demand in the long run, some firms will increase their scale of operations, and new firms will likely enter the industry. In response to a decrease in demand, the short-run equilibrium price and quantity will fall, and firms will decrease their scale of operations or exit the market in the long run.

Figure 7: Short-Run Adjustment to an Increase in Demand Under Perfect Competition

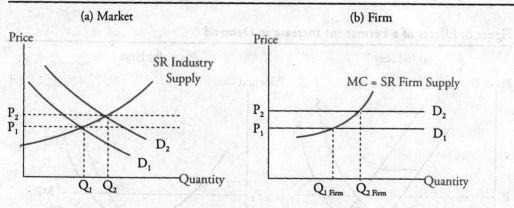

A firm's long-run adjustment to a shift in industry demand and the resulting change in price may be either to alter the size of its plant or leave the market entirely. The marketplace abounds with examples of firms that have increased their plant sizes (or added additional production facilities) to increase output in response to increasing market demand. Other firms, such as Ford and GM, have decreased plant size to reduce economic losses. This strategy is commonly referred to as *downsizing*.

If an industry is characterized by firms earning economic profits, new firms will enter the market. This will cause industry supply to increase (the industry supply curve shifts downward and to the right), increasing equilibrium output and decreasing equilibrium price. Even though industry output increases, however, individual firms will produce less because as price falls, each individual firm will move down its own supply curve. The end result is that a firm's total revenue and economic profit will decrease.

If firms in an industry are experiencing economic losses, some of these firms will exit the market. This will decrease industry supply and increase equilibrium price. Each remaining firm in the industry will move up its individual supply curve and increase production at the higher market price. This will cause total revenues to increase, reducing any economic losses the remaining firms had been experiencing.

LOS 18.d: Discuss how a permanent change in demand or changes in technology affect price, output, and economic profit.

A *permanent change in demand* leads to the entry of firms to, or exit of firms from, an industry. Let's consider the permanent increase in demand illustrated in Figure 8. The initial long-run industry equilibrium condition shown in Figure 8(a) is at the intersection of demand curve D_0 and supply curve S_0, at price P_0 and quantity Q_0. As indicated in Figure 8(b), at the market price of P_0 each firm will produce q_0. At this price and output, each firm earns a normal profit, and economic profit is zero. That is, $MC = MR = P$ and ATC is at its minimum. Now, suppose industry demand permanently increases such that the industry demand curve in Figure 8(a) shifts to D_1. The new market price will be P_1 and industry output will increase to Q_1. At the new price P_1, existing firms will produce q_1 and realize an economic profit because $P_1 >$ ATC. Positive economic profits will cause new firms to enter the market. As these new firms increase total industry supply, the industry supply curve will gradually shift to S_1, and the market price will decline back to P_0. At the market price of P_0, the industry will now produce Q_2, with an increased number of firms in the industry, each producing at the original quantity, q_0. The individual firms will no longer enjoy an economic profit because ATC $= P_0$ at q_0.

Figure 8: Effects of a Permanent Increase in Demand

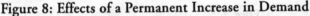

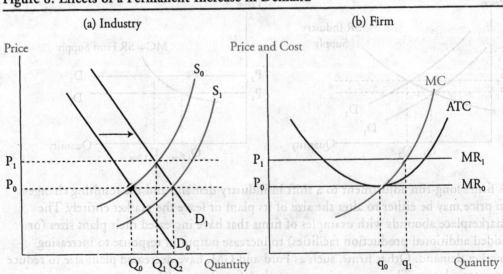

©2010 Kaplan, Inc.

The long-run equilibrium price after a permanent increase in demand may be higher or lower than before, depending on the effect of greater input purchases on input prices. In a situation referred to as **external economies of scale**, input prices fall because of the greater demand. As computer demand increased, economies of scale in producing the central processing units allowed computer makers to decrease prices, even as output increased. This effect was compounded by technological improvements in manufacturing technology. The long-run supply curve for the industry is downward sloping when external economies of scale reduce production costs for larger quantities.

External diseconomies of scale refer to a situation when the increased demand for productive inputs results in an increase in their prices. In this case, a permanent increase in market demand for the finished product will result in an increase in both equilibrium price and output. A permanent increase in the market demand for aluminum will increase the long-run equilibrium price and output of aluminum because the supply curve for bauxite (aluminum ore) is upward sloping. The long-run supply curve for the industry is upward sloping when external diseconomies of scale increase production costs as industry output expands.

In sum, the slope of the long-run industry supply curve depends on the effect of increased industry output on the prices of the important inputs in the production process. The two cases are illustrated in Figure 9. The initial price change in response to an increase in industry demand, from D_0 to D_1, is movement along the short-run supply curve (SRS_0) to a higher price in the short run (P_{SR}). In the long run, as producers enter the industry, short-run industry supply increases to SRS_1 and the shape of the long-run industry supply curve (LRS) depends on whether productive inputs are subject to economies or diseconomies of scale. With external economies (diseconomies) of scale, the long-run effect of a permanent increase in demand is an increase in output and a decrease (increase) in the equilibrium market price to P_{LR}.

Figure 9: Long-Run Industry Supply in a Competitive Market

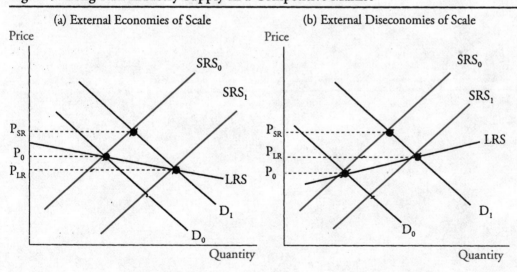

Technological changes, such as a lower-cost production process, usually require firms to invest in additional fixed assets (e.g., plant and equipment). Consequently, technological advances take some time to become common practice throughout an industry. Once individual firms have implemented technological changes, their costs decline and their supply (cost) curve shifts to the right. At the lower costs, firms are willing to supply a given quantity at a reduced price or provide more of a product at a higher price. In either case, the lower cost structure for the individual firms shifts the industry supply curve to the right. With a given demand, and this repositioned industry supply curve, the industry supplies more of a given product at a lower price.

Firms that are the first to adopt the new cost-reducing technology will earn economic profits. New firms that use the new technology will be attracted to the industry by profits. Existing firms using the older (higher-cost) technology will experience economic losses and be forced to either adopt the new technology or exit the industry. Long-run equilibrium with price equal to minimum average total cost for the new technology will be established after all firms in the industry have adopted the new technology. In long-run equilibrium, firms again will earn zero economic profits as the number of firms in the industry will be the number for which total industry supply makes equilibrium price equal to minimum average total cost (and marginal cost) for each firm.

KEY CONCEPTS

LOS 18.a

Conditions of perfectly competitive markets:

- All the firms in the market produce a homogeneous product.
- There is a large number of independent firms.
- Each seller is small relative to the total market.
- There are no barriers to entry or exit.

Price takers are firms that take the market price as given. In a perfectly competitive market, each producer is a price taker because production decisions cannot influence the market price.

Although the market demand curve is downward sloping, under perfect competition, each firm faces a perfectly elastic (horizontal) demand curve and, therefore, its marginal revenue at any output level equals the market price.

LOS 18.b

Firms maximize profits by producing the quantity for which marginal revenue equals marginal cost. Because marginal revenue for a price-taker firm is equal to the market price, price-taker firms maximize profits at the output level for which the marginal cost equals the market price.

Economic profit or loss equals total revenues less the opportunity cost (implicit and explicit costs) of production, which includes a normal profit. Economic profit is zero in the long run for a firm in a perfectly competitive market.

A price-taker firm should continue to operate if the market price is temporarily less than its average total cost but greater than its average variable cost, but the firm should shut down temporarily if price is less than average variable cost. A firm that believes price will always be less than average total cost should go out of business.

LOS 18.c

The short-run supply curve for a perfectly competitive firm is the segment of its marginal cost curve that lies above its average variable cost curve.

An increase (decrease) in market demand will increase (decrease) market price and output as individual firms increase (decrease) output and firms enter (exit) the industry in response to the change in market price, which is also marginal revenue.

In the long run, firms will adjust their scale of operations (plant size) in response to changes in market price in order to minimize average total cost at their new profit maximizing level of output.

LOS 18.d

In a perfectly competitive market, a permanent increase (decrease) in market demand and market price leads to an increase (decrease) in the number of firms operating, as new firms enter when existing firms are earning economic profits (some firms exit when existing firms are experiencing economic losses).

Firms that are among the first to adopt new cost-saving technology will expand output and earn economic profits for a period of time. When all industry firms have adopted the new technology, industry supply and equilibrium quantity will both be greater. Equilibrium price will be lower and will again be equal to both marginal cost and minimum average total cost for each firm, so economic profit returns to zero in equilibrium.

CONCEPT CHECKERS

1. A firm operating under conditions of pure competition will:
    A. face a vertical demand curve.
    B. generate zero economic profit in the long run.
    C. produce a quantity where marginal revenue is less than marginal cost.

2. Under pure competition, a firm will experience economic losses when:
    A. price is less than ATC.
    B. MC is less than ATC.
    C. MC = ATC = MR = price.

3. A price-taker firm will increase output as long as:
    A. marginal revenue is positive.
    B. marginal revenue is greater than marginal cost.
    C. marginal revenue is greater than the average cost.

4. Which of these statements is *most accurate* regarding the characteristics of a perfectly competitive market?
    A. Firms' products are different.
    B. The competitors never earn economic profits.
    C. Barriers to entry into the market are nonexistent.

5. Under perfect competition, the long-run equilibrium condition for a firm may be described as:
    A. P = ATC = TR.
    B. MC = TR = TC.
    C. P = MC = ATC.

6. When a firm operates under conditions of pure competition, marginal revenue always equals:
    A. price.
    B. average fixed cost.
    C. average variable cost.

7. A firm is likely to continue production in the short run as long as price is at least equal to:
    A. marginal cost.
    B. average total cost.
    C. average variable cost.

8. A purely competitive firm will tend to expand its output so long as:
    A. its marginal revenue is positive.
    B. the marginal revenue is greater than price.
    C. the market price is greater than marginal cost.

9. The demand for the product of a purely competitive firm is:
    A. perfectly elastic.
    B. perfectly inelastic.
    C. greater than zero but less than one.

10. In a purely competitive market, economic losses indicate that:
   A. price is below average total costs.
   B. collusion is occurring in the market place.
   C. firms need to expand output to reduce costs.

©2010 Kaplan, Inc.

ANSWERS – CONCEPT CHECKERS

1. **B** A firm operating under conditions of pure competition will generate zero economic profit in the long run. In the short run, firms may generate economic profits. However, because of the lack of entry barriers, new competitors will enter the market and prices will adjust downward until economic profits disappear.

2. **A** Under pure competition, a firm will experience losses when its selling price is less than average total cost. The other possible answers will not necessarily result in losses.

3. **B** A firm will increase output, as long as MR > MC.

     Professor's Note: Don't forget that economic profit is the firm's total revenues less its opportunity cost.

4. **C** The only true statement listed in the question is that, under pure competition, there are no barriers to entry into the market. "Competitors never earn economic profits" is incorrect because price-taker firms can earn positive economic profits in the short run.

5. **C** For a competitive firm, long-run equilibrium is where P = MC = ATC. For price-taker firms, P = MR. Competition eliminates economic profits in the long run so that P = ATC.

6. **A** When a firm operates under conditions of pure competition, MR always equals price. This is because, in pure competition, demand is perfectly elastic (a horizontal line), so MR is constant and equal to price.

7. **C** If price is greater than average variable cost, a firm will continue to operate in the short run because it is covering at least some of its fixed costs.

8. **C** A purely competitive firm will tend to expand its output so long as the market price is greater than MC. In the short term and long term, profit is maximized when P = MC.

9. **A** The demand for the product of a purely competitive firm is perfectly elastic. This is true because the market dictates price. If a price taker increases its price above the market price, the firm will sell no units.

10. **A** In a purely competitive market, economic losses indicate that firms are overproducing, causing prices to fall below average total costs. This can occur in the short run. In the long run, however, market supply will decrease as firms exit the industry, and prices will rise to the point where economic profits are zero.

Monopoly

Exam Focus

Be able to identify the key features of a monopoly and how natural monopolies arise. Know the relationship between price, marginal revenue, average cost, and marginal cost for a monopoly and why monopolies restrict output to an economically inefficient quantity compared to pure competition. Understand the social benefit of regulation imposing average cost pricing and why marginal cost pricing for a natural monopoly requires a subsidy.

LOS 19.a: Describe the characteristics of a monopoly, including factors that allow a monopoly to arise, and monopoly price-setting strategies.

A **monopoly** is characterized by one seller of a specific, well-defined product that has *no good substitutes*. For a firm to maintain its monopoly position, it must be the case that *barriers to market entry are high*.

Barriers to entry are factors that make it difficult for competing firms to enter a market. There are two types of barriers to entry that can result in a monopoly: legal barriers and natural barriers.

Legal Barriers

Most legal barriers to entry do not result in actual monopolies. Restrictions on broadcast licenses for radio and television stations granted by the Federal Communications Commission in the United States present significant barriers to entry. Within each market, however, several such licenses are granted, so no one station has a monopoly on radio or television broadcasts. Such restrictions also offer an example of how market power of firms protected from competition by legal restrictions can erode over time as substitute products are developed. The introduction of cable television, satellite television, and, most recently, satellite radio have all significantly eroded the protection offered by possessing a local broadcast license.

Patents, copyrights, and government-granted franchises are legal barriers to entry that can result in a single, monopoly producer of a good in a market. U.S. laws give the U.S. Postal Service the exclusive right to deliver mail (although substitute products have been introduced) and local laws grant exclusive rights to water, electric, and other utilities. Patents give their owners the exclusive right to produce a good for a period of years, just as copyright protection is offered to the creators of original material. Pharmaceutical firms, semiconductor firms, and software creators are a few of the types of firms that enjoy such protection from competition.

Natural Barriers

In some industries, the economics of production lead to a single firm supplying the entire market demand for the product. When there are large *economies of scale,* it means that the average cost of production decreases as a single firm produces greater and greater output. An example is an electric utility. The fixed costs of producing electricity and building the power lines and related equipment to deliver it to homes are quite high. The marginal cost of providing electricity to an additional home or of providing more electricity to a home is, however, quite low. The more electricity provided, the lower the average cost per kilowatt hour. When the average cost of production for a single firm is falling throughout the relevant range of consumer demand, we say that the industry is a **natural monopoly**. The entry of another firm into the industry would divide the production between two firms and result in a higher average cost of production than for a single producer. Thus, large economies of scale in an industry present significant barriers to entry.

A monopoly faces a downward sloping demand curve for its product, so profit maximization involves a trade-off between price and quantity sold if the firm sells at the same price to all buyers. Assuming a single selling price, a monopoly firm must lower its price in order to sell a greater quantity. Unlike a firm in perfect competition, a firm facing a downward sloping demand curve must determine what price to charge, hoping to find the price and output combination that will bring the maximum profit to the firm.

Monopoly Price-Setting Strategies

Two pricing strategies that are possible for a monopoly are *single-price* and *price discrimination.* If the monopoly's customers cannot resell the product to each other, the monopoly can maximize profits by charging different prices to different groups of customers. When price discrimination isn't possible, the monopoly will charge a single price. Price discrimination is described in more detail later in this topic.

LOS 19.b: Explain the relation between price, marginal revenue, and elasticity for a monopoly, and determine a monopoly's profit-maximizing price and quantity.

To maximize profit, monopolists will expand output until marginal revenue (MR) equals marginal cost (MC). Due to high entry barriers, monopolist profits do not attract new market entrants. Therefore, long-run positive economic profits can exist. Do monopolists charge the highest possible price? The answer is no, because monopolists want to maximize profits, not price.

Figure 1 shows the revenue-cost structure facing the monopolist. Note that production will expand until MR = MC at optimal output Q*. To find the price at which it will sell Q* units, you must go to the demand curve. The demand curve itself does not determine the optimal behavior of the monopolist. Just like the perfect competition model, the profit maximizing output for a monopolist is where MR = MC. To ensure a profit, the demand curve must lie above the firm's average total cost (ATC) curve at the optimal quantity so that price > ATC. The optimal quantity will be in the elastic range of the demand curve.

Figure 1: Monopolistic Short-Run Costs and Revenues

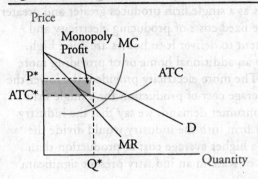

Once again, the *profit maximizing* output for a monopolistic firm is the one for which MR = MC. As shown in Figure 1, the profit maximizing output is Q*, with a price of P*, and an economic profit equal to (P* – ATC*) × Q*.

Monopolists are *price searchers* and have *imperfect information* regarding market demand. They must experiment with different prices to find the one that maximizes profit.

LOS 19.c: Explain price discrimination and why perfect price discrimination is efficient.

Price discrimination is the practice of charging different consumers different prices for the same product or service. Examples are different prices for airline tickets based on whether a Saturday-night stay is involved (separates business travelers and leisure travelers) and different prices for movie tickets based on age.

The motivation for a monopolist is to capture more consumer surplus as economic profit than is possible by charging a single price.

For price discrimination to work, the seller must:

- Face a downward-sloping demand curve.
- Have at least two identifiable groups of customers with *different price elasticities of demand* for the product.
- Be able to prevent the customers paying the lower price from reselling the product to the customers paying the higher price.

As long as these conditions are met, firm profits can be increased through price discrimination.

Figure 2 illustrates how price discrimination can increase the total quantity supplied and increase economic profits compared to a single-price pricing strategy. For simplicity, we have assumed no fixed costs and constant variable costs so that MC = ATC. In panel (a), the single profit-maximizing price is $100 at a quantity of 80 (where MC = MR), which generates a profit of $2,400. In panel (b), the firm is able to separate consumers, charges one group $110 and sells them 50 units, and sells an additional 60 units to another group (with more elastic demand) at a price of $90. Total profit is increased to $3,200, and total output is increased from 80 units to 110 units.

Compared to the quantity produced under perfect competition, the quantity produced by a monopolist reduces the sum of consumer and producer surplus by an amount represented by the triangle labeled *deadweight loss* (DWL) in panel (a) of Figure 2. Consumer surplus is reduced not only by the decrease in quantity but also by the increase in price relative to perfect competition. Monopoly is considered inefficient because the reduction in output compared to perfect competition reduces the sum of consumer and producer surplus. Because marginal benefit is greater than marginal cost, less than the efficient quantity of resources are allocated to the production of the good. Price discrimination reduces this inefficiency by increasing output toward the quantity where marginal benefit equals marginal cost. Note that the deadweight loss is smaller in panel (b). The firm gains from those customers with inelastic demand while still providing goods to customers with more elastic demand. This may even cause production to take place when it would not otherwise.

An extreme (and largely theoretical) case of price discrimination is perfect price discrimination. If it were possible for the monopolist to charge each consumer the maximum they are willing to pay for each unit, there would be no deadweight loss because a monopolist would produce the same quantity as under perfect competition. With perfect price discrimination, there would be no consumer surplus. It would all be captured by the monopolist.

Figure 2: Effect of Price Discrimination on Output and Operating Profit

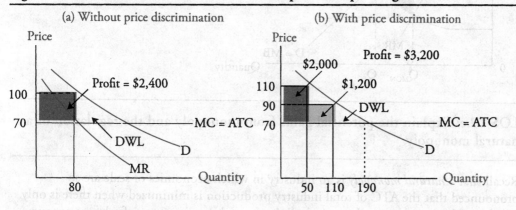

LOS 19.d: Explain how consumer and producer surplus are redistributed in a monopoly, including the occurrence of deadweight loss and rent seeking.

Figure 3 illustrates the difference in allocative efficiency between monopoly and perfect competition. Under *perfect competition*, the industry supply curve, S, is the sum of the supply curves of the many competing firms in the industry. The perfect competition equilibrium price and quantity are at the intersection of the industry supply curve and the market demand curve, D. The quantity produced is Q_{PC} at an equilibrium price P_{PC}. Because each firm is small relative to the industry, there is nothing to be gained by attempting to decrease output in an effort to increase price.

A monopolist facing the same demand curve, and with the same marginal cost curve, MC, will maximize profit by producing Q_{MON} (where MC = MR) and charging a price of P_{MON}.

The important thing to note here is that when compared to a perfectly competitive industry, the monopoly firm will produce less total output and charge a higher price.

Recall from our review of perfect competition that the efficient quantity is the one for which the sum of consumer surplus and producer surplus is maximized. In Figure 3, this quantity is where S = D, or equivalently, where marginal cost (MC) = marginal benefit (MB). *Monopoly creates a deadweight loss* relative to perfect competition because monopolies produce a quantity that does not maximize the sum of consumer surplus and producer surplus. A further loss of efficiency results from **rent seeking** when producers spend time and resources to try to acquire or establish a monopoly.

Figure 3: Perfect Competition vs. Monopoly

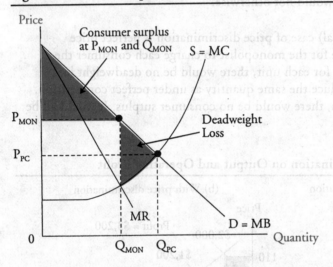

LOS 19.e: Explain the potential gains from monopoly and the regulation of a natural monopoly.

Recall that a *natural monopoly* is an industry in which economies of scale are so pronounced that the ATC of total industry production is minimized when there is only one firm. Here, average total cost is declining over the entire range of relevant outputs. Fixed costs are high and marginal costs are quite low. We illustrate the case of a natural monopoly in Figure 4. Left unregulated, a single-price monopolist will maximize profits by producing where MR = MC, producing quantity Q_U and charging P_U. Given the economies of scale, having another firm in the market would increase the ATC significantly. Note in Figure 4 that if two firms each produced approximately one-half of output Q_{AC}, average cost for each firm would be much higher than for a single producer producing Q_{AC}. Thus, there is a potential gain from monopoly because of lower average cost production when LRAC is decreasing so that economies of scale lead to a single supplier.

Figure 4: Natural Monopoly—Average Cost and Marginal Cost Pricing

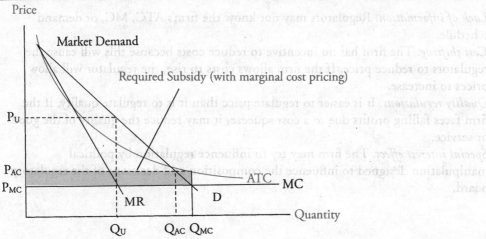

Economies of scope can also lead to a natural monopoly, especially in an industry where economies of scale also exist. Economies of scope occur when a firm expands the range of goods it produces such that its average total cost is reduced. A firm such as Boeing uses very specialized equipment and computer programs to engineer the many parts that go into an airplane. This means that it can produce these components at a lower average cost than individual suppliers could.

Regulators often attempt to increase competition and efficiency through efforts to reduce artificial barriers to trade, such as licensing requirements, quotas, and tariffs.

Because monopolists produce less than the optimal quantity (do not achieve efficient resource allocation), government regulation may be aimed at improving resource allocation by regulating the prices monopolies may charge. This may be done through **average cost pricing** or **marginal cost pricing**.

Average cost pricing is the most common form of regulation. This would result in a price of P_{AC} and an output of Q_{AC} as illustrated in Figure 4. It forces monopolists to reduce price to where the firm's ATC intersects the market demand curve. This will:

- Increase output and decrease price.
- Increase social welfare (allocative efficiency).
- Ensure the monopolist a *normal* profit because price = ATC.

Marginal cost pricing, which is also referred to as *efficient regulation*, forces the monopolist to reduce price to the point where the firm's MC curve intersects the market demand curve. This increases output and reduces price, but causes the monopolist to incur a loss because price is below ATC, as illustrated in Figure 4. Such a solution requires a government subsidy in order to provide the firm with a normal profit and prevent it from leaving the market entirely.

Regulators sometimes go astray when dealing with the problems of markets with high barriers to entry. The reasons for this include:

- *Lack of information.* Regulators may not know the firm's ATC, MC, or demand schedule.
- *Cost shifting.* The firm has no incentive to reduce costs because this will cause the regulators to reduce price. If the firm allows costs to rise, the regulator will allow prices to increase.
- *Quality regulations.* It is easier to regulate price than it is to regulate quality. If the firm faces falling profits due to a cost squeeze, it may reduce the quality of the good or service.
- *Special interest effect.* The firm may try to influence regulation by political manipulation designed to influence the composition and decisions of the regulatory board.

KEY CONCEPTS

LOS 19.a

Monopoly is characterized by one seller of a specific, well-defined product that has no good substitutes and high barriers to entry. Barriers to entry include economies of scale, government licensing and legal barriers, patents or exclusive rights of production, and resource control.

Monopoly price-setting strategies include charging a single profit-maximizing price and price discrimination, where different prices are charged to different groups of customers.

LOS 19.b

Like all firms, monopolists maximize profits by producing the quantity where marginal revenue equals marginal cost.

Monopolists are price searchers (face downward sloping demand curves) and have imperfect information about demand, so they must experiment with different prices (search) to find the profit maximizing price/quantity. This price/quantity will always be in the elastic range of the demand curve for the firm's product.

LOS 19.c

Price discrimination can increase both output and monopoly profits only if there are at least two identifiable groups of customers with different price elasticities of demand, and the monopolist can prevent lower-price-paying customers from reselling to higher-price-paying customers.

If a monopolist were able to charge the maximum price each consumer would pay (perfect price discrimination), the output quantity would be efficient since output is at the level where marginal social benefit equals marginal social cost, but all consumer surplus would be captured by the monopolist.

LOS 19.d

Compared to perfect competition, monopolists that are unable to practice perfect price discrimination produce less than the efficient level of output. While this results in a deadweight loss to society, producer surplus is greater since the monopolist is able to capture more of what would be consumer surplus under perfect competition. Monopolists are willing to devote resources to achieving and maintaining a monopoly and capture economic profit (monopoly rents). This is termed rent seeking.

LOS 19.e

A natural monopoly exists when economies of scale are so pronounced that average total cost is falling (MC < ATC) over the entire relevant output range so that the cost of total industry production is minimized when there is only one firm in the industry.

Regulation of a natural monopoly can take the form of average cost pricing or marginal cost pricing.

- With average cost pricing, the most common form of regulation, regulators require a natural monopoly to charge a price equal to average total cost, where the market demand curve intersects the average total cost curve.

- Marginal cost pricing (efficient regulation) forces a monopolist to charge a price equal to marginal cost, where the firm's marginal cost curve intersects the market demand curve. This increases output and reduces price but requires a government subsidy since price (marginal cost) is then less than average total cost.

CONCEPT CHECKERS

1. A monopolist will expand production until MR = MC and charge a price determined by the:
    A. demand curve.
    B. marginal cost curve.
    C. average total cost curve.

2. Which of the following statements *most accurately* describes a significant difference between a monopoly firm and a perfectly competitive firm? A perfectly competitive firm:
    A. minimizes costs; a monopolistic firm maximizes profit.
    B. maximizes profit; a monopolistic firm maximizes price.
    C. takes price as given; a monopolistic firm must search for the best price.

3. A natural monopoly may exist when:
    A. ATC increases as output increases.
    B. economies of scale are great.
    C. all production is divided between just a few firms.

4. A monopolist will maximize profits by producing at the output level where:
    A. price is equal to MC.
    B. MR equals ATC and charging a price along the demand curve that corresponds to the output rate.
    C. MR equals MC and charging a price on the demand curve that corresponds to the output rate.

5. For effective price discrimination to occur, the seller must:
    A. face a downward-sloping demand curve.
    B. have a large advertising budget relative to sales.
    C. be able to ensure resale of the product among customers.

6. A monopoly situation in which the ATC of production steadily declines with increased output is called a:
    A. natural monopoly.
    B. structural monopoly.
    C. declining cost monopoly.

7. When a regulatory agency requires a monopolist to use average cost pricing, the intent is to price the product where the:
    A. MR curve intersects the demand curve.
    B. ATC curve intersects the MR curve.
    C. ATC curve intersects the market demand curve.

ANSWERS – CONCEPT CHECKERS

1. **A** A monopolist will expand production until MR = MC, and the price of the product will be determined by the demand curve.

2. **C** Monopolists must search for the profit maximizing price (and output) because they do not have perfect information regarding demand. Firms under perfect competition take the market price as given and only determine the profit maximizing quantity.

3. **B** A natural monopoly may exist when economies of scale are great. The large economies of scale make it inefficient to have multiple producers.

4. **C** A monopolist will maximize profits by producing at the output level where MR equals MC and charging a price on the demand curve that corresponds to the output rate. This will maximize profits. The goal of the monopolist is to maximize profits, not price or revenue.

5. **A** In order for effective price discrimination to occur, the seller must face a downward-sloping demand curve. The seller must also have at least two identifiable groups of customers with different price elasticities of demand for the product, and the seller must be able to *prevent* customers from reselling the product.

6. **A** A monopoly situation in which the ATC of production continually declines with increased output is called a natural monopoly.

7. **C** When a regulatory agency requires a monopolist to use average cost pricing, the intent is to price the product where the ATC curve intersects the market demand curve. A problem in using this method is actually determining exactly what the ATC is.

The following is a review of the Economics principles designed to address the learning outcome statements set forth by CFA Institute®. This topic is also covered in:

MONOPOLISTIC COMPETITION AND OLIGOPOLY

EXAM FOCUS

Make sure you know the characteristics of both of these types of markets. For monopolistic competition, know the importance of advertising, product differentiation, and product innovation and arguments about the economic efficiency of these activities. Be able to explain how firms in monopolistic competition earn economic profits in the short run and how output and price are determined in the long run. Understand the incentives of oligopolists to collude and how the Prisoners' Dilemma relates to oligopoly output decisions when two firms enter into a price-fixing agreement.

LOS 20.a: Describe the characteristics of monopolistic competition and an oligopoly.

Monopolistic competition has the following market characteristics:

- *A large number of independent sellers*: (1) Each firm has a relatively small market share, so no individual firm has any significant power over price. (2) Firms need only pay attention to average market price, not the price of individual competitors. (3) There are too many firms in the industry for collusion (price fixing) to be possible.
- *Differentiated products*: Each producer has a product that is slightly different from its competitors (at least in the minds of consumers). The competing products are close substitutes for one another.
- *Firms compete on price, quality, and marketing* as a result of product differentiation. *Quality* is a significant product-differentiating characteristic. *Price* and output can be set by firms because they face downward-sloping demand curves, but there is usually a strong correlation between quality and the price that firms can charge. *Marketing* is a must to inform the market about a product's (differentiating) characteristics.
- *Low barriers to entry* so that firms are free to enter and exit the market. If firms in the industry are earning economic profits, new firms can be expected to enter the industry.

Firms in monopolistic competition face *downward-sloping demand* curves (they are price searchers). Their demand curves are highly *elastic* because competing products are perceived by consumers as close substitutes. Think about the market for toothpaste. All toothpaste is quite similar, but differentiation occurs due to taste preferences, influential advertising, and the reputation of the seller. However, if the price of your favorite brand increased significantly, you would be more likely to try other brands, which you would likely not do if the prices of all brands were similar.

Oligopoly is a form of market competition characterized by:

- A small number of sellers.
- Interdependence among competitors (decisions made by one firm affect the demand, price, and profit of others in the industry).
- Significant barriers to entry that often include large economies of scale.
- Products that may be similar *or* differentiated.

In contrast to a monopolist, *oligopolists are highly dependent upon the actions of their rivals* when making business decisions. Price determination in the auto industry is a good example. Automakers tend to play "follow the leader" and announce price increases or decreases in close synchronization. They are *not* working explicitly together, but the actions of one producer have a large impact on the others. In addition, the barriers to entry are high in oligopoly markets. The enormous capital investment necessary to start a new auto company or airplane manufacturing firm, because of the large economies of scale in those industries, poses a significant barrier to entry.

LOS 20.b: Determine the profit-maximizing (loss-minimizing) output under monopolistic competition, explain why long-run economic profit under monopolistic competition is zero, and determine if monopolistic competition is efficient.

LOS 20.c: Compare and contrast monopolistic competition and perfect competition.

The price/output decision for monopolistic competition is illustrated in Figure 1. Panel (a) of Figure 1 illustrates the short-run price/output characteristics of monopolistic competition for a single firm. As indicated, firms in monopolistic competition maximize economic profits by producing where marginal revenue (MR) equals marginal cost (MC), and by charging the price for that quantity from the demand curve, D. Here the firm earns positive economic profits because price, P^*, exceeds average total cost (ATC^*). Due to low barriers to entry, competitors will enter the market in pursuit of these economic profits.

Panel (b) of Figure 1 illustrates long-run equilibrium for a *representative* firm after new firms have entered the market. As indicated, the entry of new firms shifts the demand curve faced by each individual firm down to the point where price equals average total cost ($P^* = ATC^*$), such that economic profit is zero. At this point, there is no longer an incentive for new firms to enter the market, and long-run equilibrium is established. The firm in monopolistic competition continues to produce at the quantity where MR = MC but no longer earns positive economic profits.

Figure 1: Short-Run and Long-Run Output Under Monopolistic Competition

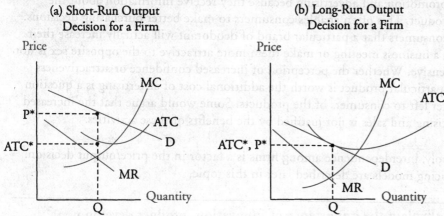

(a) Short-Run Output
Decision for a Firm

(b) Long-Run Output
Decision for a Firm

Figure 2 illustrates the differences between long-run equilibrium in markets with monopolistic competition and markets with perfect competition. Note that with monopolistic competition, price is greater than marginal cost (i.e., producers can realize a **markup**), average total cost is not at a minimum for the quantity produced (suggesting **excess capacity**, or an inefficient scale of production), and the price is slightly higher than under perfect competition. The point to consider here, however, is that perfect competition is characterized by no product differentiation. The question of the efficiency of monopolistic competition becomes, "Is there an economically efficient amount of product differentiation?"

In a world with only one brand of toothpaste, clearly average production costs would be lower. That fact alone probably does not mean that a world with only one brand/type of toothpaste would be a better world. While product differentiation has costs, it also has benefits to consumers. As we will see in the next section, additional benefits in terms of greater product innovation and the information about quality that can be conveyed by brand names may also offset the apparent lack of efficiency in markets characterized by monopolistic competition.

Figure 2: Firm Output Under Monopolistic and Perfect Competition

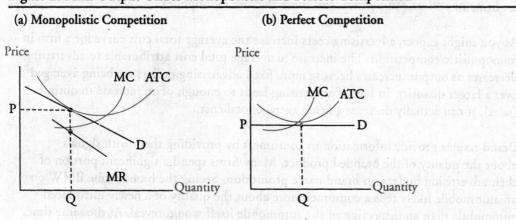

(a) Monopolistic Competition

(b) Perfect Competition

Efficiency of monopolistic competition is unclear. Consumers definitely benefit from brand name promotion and advertising because they receive information about the nature of a product. This often enables consumers to make better purchasing decisions. Convincing consumers that a particular brand of deodorant will actually increase their confidence in a business meeting or make them more attractive to the opposite sex is not easy or inexpensive. Whether the perception of increased confidence or attractiveness from using a particular product is worth the additional cost of advertising is a question probably better left to consumers of the products. Some would argue that the increased cost of advertising and sales is not justified by the benefits of these activities.

For an oligopoly, interdependence among firms is a factor in the price/output decision. Oligopoly pricing models are described later in this topic.

LOS 20.d: Explain the importance of innovation, product development, advertising, and branding under monopolistic competition.

Product innovation is a necessary activity as firms in monopolistic competition pursue economic profits. Firms that bring new and innovative products to the market are confronted with less-elastic demand curves, enabling them to increase price and earn economic profits. However, close substitutes and imitations will eventually erode the initial economic profit from an innovative product. Thus, firms in monopolistic competition must continually look for innovative product features that will make their products relatively more desirable to some consumers than those of the competition.

Innovation does not come without costs. The costs of product innovation must be weighed against the extra revenue that it produces. A firm is considered to be spending the optimal amount on innovation when the marginal cost of (additional) innovation just equals the marginal revenue (marginal benefit) of additional innovation.

Advertising expenses are high for firms in monopolistic competition. This is to inform consumers about the unique features of their products and to create or increase a perception of differences between products that are actually quite similar. We just note here that advertising costs for firms in monopolistic competition are greater than those for firms in perfect competition and those that are monopolies.

As you might expect, advertising costs increase the average total cost curve for a firm in monopolistic competition. The increase to average total cost attributable to advertising decreases as output increases because more fixed advertising dollars are being averaged over a larger quantity. In fact, if advertising leads to enough of an increase in output (sales), it can actually decrease a firm's average total cost.

Brand names provide information to consumers by providing them with signals about the quality of the branded product. Many firms spend a significant portion of their advertising budget on brand name promotion. Seeing the brand name BMW on an automobile likely tells a consumer more about the quality of a newly introduced automobile than an inspection of the automobile itself would reveal. At the same time, the reputation BMW has for high quality is so valuable that the firm has an added incentive not to damage it by producing vehicles of low quality.

LOS 20.e: Explain the kinked demand curve model and the dominant firm model, and determine the profit-maximizing (loss-minimizing) output under each model.

One traditional model of oligopoly, the **kinked demand curve model**, is based on the assumption that an increase in a firm's product price will not be followed by its competitors, but a decrease in price will. According to the kinked demand curve model, each firm believes that it faces a demand curve that is more elastic (flatter) above a given price (the kink in the demand curve) than it is below the given price. The kinked demand curve model is illustrated in Figure 3. The "kink" price is at price P_K, where a firm produces Q_K. A firm believes that if it raises its price above P_K, its competitors will remain at P_K, and it will lose market share because it has the highest price. Above P_K, the demand curve is considered to be relatively elastic, where a small price increase will result in a large decrease in demand. On the other hand, if a firm decreases its price below P_K, other firms will match the price cut, and all firms will experience a relatively small increase in sales relative to any price reduction. Therefore, Q_K is the profit-maximizing level of output.

Figure 3: Kinked Demand Curve Model

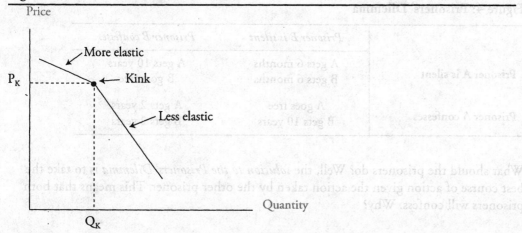

Another traditional oligopoly model, the **dominant firm oligopoly model**, is based on the assumptions that one of the firms in an oligopoly market has a significant cost advantage over its competitors and that this dominant firm produces a relatively large proportion of the industry's output. Under this model, the dominant firm resembles a monopoly, with a marginal revenue curve below the demand curve. The dominant firm produces the quantity of output at which its marginal revenue equals its marginal cost. The rest of the firms in the industry are essentially price takers, producing the quantity at which their marginal cost equals the price set by the dominant firm.

LOS 20.f: Describe oligopoly games including the Prisoners' Dilemma.

Game theory is used to examine strategic behavior in an oligopoly. **Prisoners' Dilemma** is a simple game that may be used to describe the decisions faced by firms competing under oligopoly conditions. Prisoners' Dilemma may be described as follows:

Two prisoners, A and B, are believed to have committed a serious crime. However, the prosecutor does not feel that the police have sufficient evidence for a conviction. The prisoners are separated and offered the following deal:

- If Prisoner A confesses and Prisoner B remains silent, Prisoner A goes free and Prisoner B receives a 10-year prison sentence.
- If Prisoner B confesses and Prisoner A remains silent, Prisoner B goes free and Prisoner A receives a 10-year prison sentence.
- If both prisoners remain silent, each will receive a 6-month sentence.
- If both prisoners confess, each will receive a 2-year sentence.

Each prisoner must choose either to betray the other by confessing or to remain silent. Neither prisoner, however, knows for sure what the other prisoner will choose to do. The result for each of these four possible outcomes is presented in Figure 4.

Figure 4: Prisoners' Dilemma

	Prisoner B is silent	*Prisoner B confesses*
Prisoner A is silent	A gets 6 months B gets 6 months	A gets 10 years B goes free
Prisoner A confesses	A goes free B gets 10 years	A gets 2 years B gets 2 years

What should the prisoners do? Well, the *solution to the Prisoners' Dilemma* is to take the best course of action given the action taken by the other prisoner. This means that both prisoners will confess. Why?

Consider Prisoner B's choices. If Prisoner A remains silent, Prisoner B's best option is to confess and go free. If Prisoner A confesses, Prisoner B's best option is to confess and get two years instead of ten. So in either case, Prisoner B's best option is to confess. A similar analysis reveals that confessing is Prisoner's A best option as well. The dilemma is that both prisoners know that if they both remain silent, they will only receive a 6-month sentence, but neither has any way of knowing what the other will do.

Oligopoly firms are in a Prisoners' Dilemma type of situation because they can each earn a greater profit if they agree to share a restricted output quantity, but only if neither cheats on the agreement. Oligopolists maximize their total profits by joining together (colluding) and operating as a single seller (monopolist).

Collusion is when firms make an agreement among themselves to avoid various competitive practices, particularly price competition (e.g., by forming a **cartel** in which the firms all act as a monopoly). Figure 5 illustrates a 2-firm oligopoly with the potential for collusion.

Figure 5: Cost and Demand for 2-Firm Industry

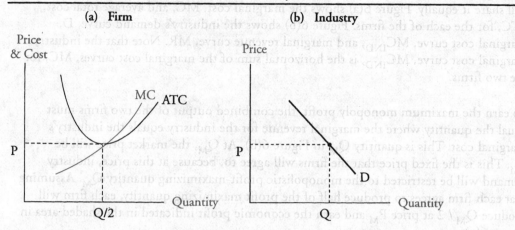

Let's assume that Firm A and Firm B are only two firms in an oligopoly market, and they each produce half of the industry's output of an identical product. Figure 5(a) shows that each of these firms produces quantity Q / 2 at price P, where marginal cost, MC, equals the minimum average total cost, ATC. Figure 5(b) is the industry demand curve, D, where Q is the quantity demanded at price P.

Now, let's assume that Firm A and Firm B have entered into an agreement to reduce output and earn increased profits. As in the Prisoners' Dilemma, these firms have two possible strategies—to honor the agreement or to cheat—so there are four possible outcomes:

• Each firm honors the agreement.
• Both firms cheat.
• Firm A honors the agreement while Firm B cheats.
• Firm B honors the agreement while Firm A cheats.

Let's examine the economic implications of each of these outcomes. Figure 6 illustrates the profit maximizing price and quantity if Firm A and Firm B collude and act jointly as if they were a single monopoly firm.

Figure 6: Price Fixing to Earn Monopoly Profits

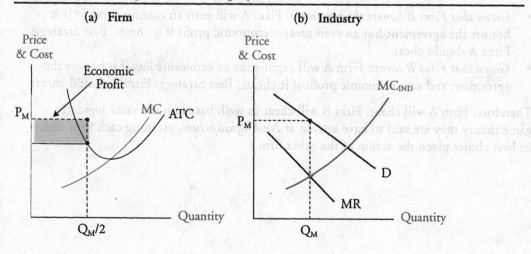

If both firms honor the contract, total economic profit will be maximized, and both firms will share it equally. Figure 6(a) shows the marginal cost, MC, and average total cost, ATC, for the each of the firms. Figure 6(b) shows the industry's demand curve, D, marginal cost curve, MC_{IND}, and marginal revenue curve, MR. Note that the industry marginal cost curve, MC_{IND}, is the horizontal sum of the marginal cost curves, MC, for the two firms.

To earn the maximum monopoly profit, the combined output of the two firms must equal the quantity where the marginal revenue for the industry equals the industry's marginal cost. This is quantity Q_M in Figure 6(b). At Q_M, the market price will be P_M. This is the fixed price that the firms will agree to, because at this price, industry demand will be restricted to the monopolistic profit-maximizing quantity Q_M. Assuming that each firm agrees to produce half of the profit maximizing quantity, each firm will produce $Q_M / 2$ at price P_M and earn the economic profit indicated in the shaded area in Figure 6(a).

If one firm cheats on the agreement by increasing output above its agreed-upon share, the total economic profit to the industry will be less than that of a monopoly, but the economic profit to the cheating firm will be greater than it would have realized when both firms honored the agreement. On the other hand, the firm that honors the agreement will now be producing the agreed-upon quantity at the same average total cost, but selling at a lower price than expected. This firm may believe that demand has fallen and that the equilibrium price for the agreed-upon total output has fallen. So, the firm that honors the agreement will experience an economic loss. However, the firm that cheated on the agreement by increasing output will realize an increased economic profit by selling more at the lower price, but at a lower average total cost. Total economic profit to the industry will decline.

If both firms cheat by increasing quantity, each firm will increase output to the point where price equals marginal cost and average total cost. The resulting price and output will approach that of a perfectly competitive industry.

Figure 7 presents the possible outcomes of the collusive agreement between Firm A and Firm B. As in the Prisoners' Dilemma, they will both cheat. Why? Consider the following argument for Firm A.

- *Given that Firm B honors the agreement:* Firm A will earn an economic profit if it honors the agreement but an even greater economic profit if it cheats. Best Strategy: Firm A should cheat.
- *Given that Firm B cheats:* Firm A will experience an economic loss if it honors the agreement and zero economic profit if it cheats. Best Strategy: Firm A should cheat.

Therefore, Firm A will cheat. Firm B will cheat as well, based on the same logic. (In game theory they are said to have arrived at *Nash equilibrium*, meaning each firm makes its best choice given the action of the other firm.)

Figure 7: Prisoners' Dilemma for Two Firms

	Firm B honors	*Firm B cheats*
Firm A honors	A earns economic profit B earns economic profit	A has an economic loss B earns increased economic profit
Firm A cheats	A earns increased economic profit B has an economic loss	A earns zero economic profit B earns zero economic profit

The probability of successful collusion is greater when cheating is easy to detect, when there are fewer oligopoly firms in a market, when the threat of new entrants to the market is less, and when enforcement of anti-collusion laws and penalties for colluding are weaker.

KEY CONCEPTS

LOS 20.a

Monopolistic competition is characterized by a large number of independent sellers, low barriers to entry, differentiated products, and firms that compete on the basis of price, quality, and marketing.

Oligopoly is a market structure characterized by a small number of sellers, interdependence among competitors (i.e., decisions made by one firm affect the demand, price, and profit of others in the industry), significant barriers to entry that often include large economies of scale, and products that may be similar or differentiated.

LOS 20.b

Firms in monopolistic competition maximize profits by producing the quantity where marginal revenue equals marginal cost and by charging the price from the demand curve.

Long-run economic profit is zero under monopolistic competition because barriers to entry are low and new firms will enter the market if existing firms are earning economic profits.

To judge whether monopolistic competition is efficient, the cost of advertising and brand name promotion must be weighed against the benefits they produce for consumers.

LOS 20.c

Producers in monopolistic competition may charge a price greater than marginal cost and produce a quantity less than the quantity at which average total cost is at a minimum. In a perfectly competitive market, price equals marginal cost, and average total cost is at a minimum for each producer.

LOS 20.d

Product innovation and development, advertising, and branding are all common for firms in monopolistic competition. New and innovative products can generate economic profits in the short run, but economic profits will erode in the long run as competitors introduce imitations and substitutes. Companies must advertise and develop brand names to differentiate their products from those of their competitors.

LOS 20.e

The kinked demand model of oligopoly is based on an assumption that each firm believes a price decrease will be matched by competitors, while a price increase will not; that is, demand is more elastic in response to a price increase than to a price decrease.

The dominant firm model of oligopoly is based on an assumption that one firm is the low-cost producer in the industry and, thus, has the ability to effectively set the market price, which higher-cost producers then take as given.

LOS 20.f

Prisoners' Dilemma is a theoretical game that illustrates that the best course of action for an oligopoly firm that has entered into an agreement with another firm to restrict their individual outputs is to cheat on the agreement and produce more than the agreed-upon amount.

©2010 Kaplan, Inc.

CONCEPT CHECKERS

1. A characteristic of monopolistic competition is:
    A. differentiated products.
    B. high barriers to entry and exit.
    C. a single seller with no competition.

2. The demand for products from monopolistic competitors is elastic due to:
    A. high barriers to entry.
    B. the availability of many close substitutes.
    C. the availability of many complementary goods.

3. Which of the following is *least likely* a feature that monopolistic competition and perfect competition have in common?
    A. Output occurs where MR = MC.
    B. Zero economic profits in the long run.
    C. Extensive advertising to differentiate products.

4. An oligopolistic industry has:
    A. few barriers to entry.
    B. few economies of scale.
    C. a great deal of interdependence among firms.

5. Consider a firm in an oligopoly market that believes the demand curve for its product is more elastic above a certain price than below this price. This belief fits *most closely* to which of the following models?
    A. Dominant firm model.
    B. Kinked demand model.
    C. Variable elasticity model.

6. Consider an agreement between France and Germany that will restrict wine production so that maximum economic profit can be realized. The possible outcomes of the agreement are presented in the table below.

	Germany complies	*Germany defaults*
France complies	France gets €8 billion Germany gets €8 billion	France gets €2 billion Germany gets €10 billion
France defaults	France gets €10 billion Germany gets €2 billion	France gets €4 billion Germany gets €4 billion

    Based on the game theory framework, the *most likely* strategy followed by the two countries with respect to whether they comply with or default on the agreement will be:
    A. both countries will default.
    B. both countries will comply.
    C. one country will default and the other will comply.

ANSWERS – CONCEPT CHECKERS

1. **A** Differentiated products are a key characteristic of monopolistic competition.

2. **B** The demand for products from firms competing in monopolistic competition is elastic due to the availability of many close substitutes. If a firm increases its product price, it will lose customers to firms selling substitute products at lower prices.

3. **C** The only item listed in the question that monopolistic competition and perfect competition do not have in common is the use of advertising to differentiate their products.

4. **C** An oligopolistic industry has a great deal of interdependence among firms. One firm's pricing decisions or advertising activities will affect the other firms.

5. **B** The kinked demand model assumes that each firm in a market believes that at some price, demand is more elastic for a price increase than for a price decrease.

6. **A** The solution for the game is for each nation to pursue the strategy that is best, given the strategy that is pursued by the other nation.
    *   Given that Germany complies with the agreement: France will get €8 billion if it complies, but €10 billion if it defaults. Therefore, France should default.
    *   Given that Germany defaults: France will get €2 billion if it complies, but €4 billion if it defaults. Therefore, France should default.
    *   Because France is better off in either case by defaulting, France will default.
    *   Germany will follow the same logic and reach the same conclusion.

The following is a review of the Economics principles designed to address the learning outcome statements set forth by CFA Institute®. This topic is also covered in:

MARKETS FOR FACTORS OF PRODUCTION

Study Session 5

EXAM FOCUS

Here, you want to gain an understanding of how the demand for inputs to production is determined and which factors influence the elasticity of demand for inputs, especially labor. The second key topic is how the market for financial capital establishes the price (interest rate) for financial capital and the factors that influence the supply of, and demand for, financial capital. Finally, you should gain an understanding of two components of the payments to productive resources, opportunity cost, and economic rent.

LOS 21.a: Explain why demand for the factors of production is called derived demand, differentiate between marginal revenue and marginal revenue product (MRP), and describe how the MRP determines the demand for labor and the wage rate.

The demand for a productive resource depends on the demand for the final goods that it is being used to produce. Thus, demand for a factor of production is a **derived demand**.

The **marginal product** of a resource is the additional output of a final product produced by using one more unit of a productive input (resource) and holding the quantities of other inputs constant. This is measured in output units and is sometimes called the marginal physical product of the resource. The **marginal revenue** is the addition to total revenue from selling one more unit of output. For a price taker, marginal revenue is equal to price. For a producer facing a downward sloping demand curve, marginal revenue is less than price, because price must be reduced in order to sell additional units of output.

The **marginal revenue product** (MRP) is the addition to total revenue gained by selling the marginal product (additional output) from employing one more unit of a productive resource. The interpretation of MRP is that it is the addition to total revenue from selling the additional output produced by using one more unit of a productive input, holding the quantities of other inputs constant.

The MRP is downward-sloping in any range of output for which diminishing marginal returns are realized from using additional units of a productive resource. This downward-sloping MRP curve is in fact the firm's short-run demand curve for the productive resource or input, as illustrated in Figure 1. This is true of any productive input, of which labor is one.

Figure 1: Marginal Revenue Product (Demand for a Productive Resource)

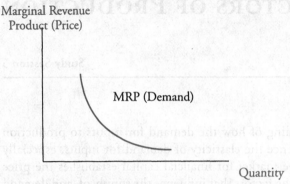

The intuition here is that a profit-maximizing firm will be willing to pay an amount for one more unit of labor (e.g., one more employee day) equal to the addition to total revenue from employing that additional labor in the production process and selling the resulting additional output. The condition for maximizing profits with respect to hiring additional units of labor is to continue to add additional units of labor until:

$$MRP_{labor} = price_{labor}$$

Once this condition is met, at any level of production that employed less labor (holding other inputs constant), there would be additional profits to be made. One more unit of labor would cost less than the value of the additional output from hiring an additional unit of labor (the MRP_{labor}). For additional units of labor beyond the amount that satisfies $MRP_{labor} = price_{labor}$, each unit of labor costs more than the additional revenue gained from the output of that unit of labor. Thus, the MRP of labor determines the equilibrium **wage rate**, the highest price a firm will pay to hire an additional unit of labor.

So we can say that a profit-maximizing firm will use additional units of a productive resource as long as its MRP is greater than its price. This supports the conclusion that the MRP curve is a firm's short-run demand curve for a productive resource (short-run, because quantities of other factors are held fixed).

LOS 21.b: Describe the factors that cause changes in the demand for labor and the factors that determine the elasticity of the demand for labor.

Now that we understand how a profit-maximizing firm determines the optimal quantity of an input to employ, we can examine the factors that will influence the firm's **demand for labor.**

An increase (decrease) in the price of the firm's output will increase (decrease) the demand for labor. An increase in the product price will increase the firm's marginal revenue, which increases the MRP of labor, increasing the demand for labor at each wage level [i.e., the demand curve for labor (the MRP curve) shifts upward]. A decrease in the price of the firm's output will have the opposite effect, by the same logic.

The effect on the demand for labor of a change in the price of another factor of production will depend on whether that factor is a complement to labor or a substitute for it. The decrease in the price of computers over time has decreased the demand for many types of labor for which a computer is a substitute (e.g., customer service personnel). The demand for IT professionals, however, has increased tremendously because they are a complement to computers in the production of the final good.

This example also illustrates the effect of technological improvements on the demand for labor. Demand for some types of labor has increased and the demand for other types of labor has decreased. Over time, the effect of technological improvements has been a net increase in the demand for labor. A rising real wage rate (wage rate adjusted for inflation) over time has provided evidence of this.

Elasticity of Demand for Labor

The demand for labor, like other types of demand, is more elastic in the long run than in the short run. This is simply because we define the short run in production as a period over which the quantities of other factors of production are fixed. If the wage rate rises, we will see a greater decrease in the quantity of labor employed when the firm can substitute (demand) other factors of production for labor (e.g., get more automated machinery).

The elasticity of labor will be greater for firms with production processes that are more labor-intensive. A warehouse operation that relies heavily on manpower to fill and ship orders will have a relatively elastic demand for labor because labor represents a large proportion of the total cost of the service it provides. For an airline, on the other hand, labor costs represent a much smaller proportion of total costs. We would expect the airline's demand for pilots to be much less elastic than a warehouse operation's demand for workers.

A third factor affecting the elasticity of demand for labor is the degree to which labor and capital can be substituted. While airplanes may, one day, have the technology to fly themselves, pilots are actually quite difficult to replace with automation (as are flight attendants). In contrast, warehouse operations and manufacturing assembly plants have found many ways to substitute capital for labor through automation and robotics. The elasticity of demand for assembly workers is much more elastic than the demand for airline pilots and flight attendants as a result of this difference in the opportunities to substitute capital for labor in production.

LOS 21.c: Describe the factors determining the supply of labor, including the substitution and income effects, and discuss the factors related to changes in the supply of labor, including capital accumulation.

Each individual decides whether, and how much, to work. Typically, labor has disutility; people generally prefer less work (and more leisure). Employers must offer a wage rate high enough that workers give up leisure time in favor of employment.

Wages, then, are the opportunity cost of leisure. The higher the wage rate, the more hours of leisure a worker will forego and the more hours of labor he will supply. This is the **substitution effect** in labor supply: workers substitute labor for leisure to the extent that the wage rate is high enough to give them an incentive to do so.

At some point, however, an individual reaches a maximum amount of labor that he is willing to offer for any wage. Just as labor has disutility, leisure has a positive value. As a worker's income increases, his demand for the things he values also increases, and leisure is one of those things. Thus an **income effect** limits how much labor a worker is willing to substitute for leisure. For the labor market as a whole, the substitution effect causes the labor supply curve to slope upward, but the income effect makes the curve bend backward at some (maximum) quantity of labor supplied.

Factors other than the wage rate that affect the supply of labor (shift the labor supply curve) include the *size of the adult population*, and *capital accumulation* in items that increase productivity in the home so that a greater proportion of adults choose to work outside the home.

LOS 21.d: Describe the effects on wages of labor unions and of a monopsony and explain the possible consequences for a market that offers an efficient wage.

Labor unions are organized so that workers can bargain for wages and other aspects of employment as a group, a process called **collective bargaining**. One way to do this is to simply restrict supply by refusing to work (striking) until the employer agrees to the new higher wage rate. This is illustrated in Figure 2. Supply of labor curve S_0 represents the supply of labor without union bargaining. With collective bargaining, the union may shift the supply curve to S_1. The result is that the wage rises from W_C to W_U, but fewer workers are employed (Q_U instead of the competitive result, Q_C).

Figure 2: Supply of Labor Restricted by Unionization

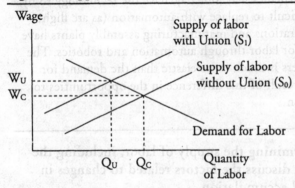

In addition to restricting supply through collective bargaining, unions attempt to increase the demand for the labor of their members in various ways. By increasing the demand for union labor, unions can reduce the decline in the quantity of union labor employed caused by the increase in the union wage rate.

One way to increase the demand for the labor of union members is to increase the marginal product of their members through additional training.

Two other ways to increase the demand for union labor are based on increasing the demand for products made by union workers. Advertisements that encourage people to buy products labeled as made by unionized employees are an example of this strategy. Another strategy is to influence trade restrictions on imported goods. Restrictions on imported steel, for example, increase the demand for domestically produced steel, which increases the demand for unionized steel workers.

Other strategies for increasing the demand for union labor are based on reducing the supply (increasing the price) of substitutes for union labor. Unions attempt to get increases in the minimum wage rate for unskilled workers because unskilled labor may be a substitute for skilled union labor. An increase in the price of a substitute productive resource (input) will increase the demand for a productive resource. Political activity centered on restricting immigrant or guest foreign workers will have the same effect because less-skilled immigrant labor is also seen as a substitute for skilled union labor.

Monopsony refers to a situation where the buyer of a good or productive input has market power, a situation opposite to that of monopoly, where the seller has market power. If an employer pays a single wage rate, increasing this wage in order to hire additional workers means that all workers receive the increased wage. The result of this is that the addition to total cost associated with hiring an additional worker is more than simply the (increased) wage for the additional worker. An employer that is the only major employer in a geographic area can face labor supply and associated marginal costs of hiring additional workers illustrated in Figure 3. A monopsonist employer will hire fewer workers, Q_M, compared to the competitive level of employment, Q_C. The employer hires workers up to the point where the marginal cost of hiring an additional worker is equal to the additional worker's MRP, but pays only the wage necessary to hire that quantity of workers, W_M. Compared to the competitive equilibrium, this is inefficient and results in a deadweight loss from underemployment, because the marginal revenue product of an additional worker is greater than the wage rate.

Figure 3: Monopsony in the Market for Labor

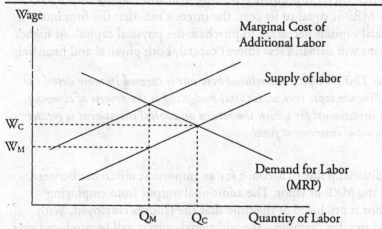

If workers are unionized and bargain collectively (as a monopoly supplier) and the employer represents a significant portion of the local demand for labor (acts as a monopsonist), the actual wage rate and employment level will be the result of bargaining between the company and the union. The wage rate will likely be somewhere between the wage rate (too high) resulting from the union's reduction in the supply of labor and the wage rate (too low) that would result if workers did not negotiate collectively and the employer paid the monopsony wage.

LOS 21.e: Differentiate between physical capital and financial capital and explain the relation between the demand for physical capital and the demand for financial capital.

Physical capital is the physical assets of a firm, including property, plant, and equipment, as well as its inventory of finished goods and goods in process. The greater the demand for physical capital, the greater the demand for the **financial capital** (money raised through issuing securities) necessary to purchase the physical capital.

A firm employs physical capital as a factor of production because it is necessary to produce the firm's output and meet customer orders. We can think, in a simple sense, of two primary factors of production: labor (people) and physical capital (machines and goods). In this sense, just as a profit-maximizing firm equates the MRP_{labor} to the wage rate, it will also equate the $MRP_{capital}$ to the cost of capital. Because the production of capital assets comes over many periods, the $MRP_{capital}$ is actually a future MRP. The value to the firm of the assets' production is the *present value* of its future MRP.

The cost of capital relevant to this decision is the cost of the funds that the firm must raise to buy physical capital. Just think of the $MRP_{capital}$ as the returns over time (in percentage terms) on the funds necessary to purchase additional physical capital. Viewed in this way, we can say that the future $MRP_{capital}$ must equal the interest rate the firm must pay to raise the financial capital in order to maximize profits.

LOS 21.f: Explain the factors that influence the demand and supply of capital.

Similar to the demand for labor, the **demand for capital** will be a downward-sloping curve derived from its MRP curve. A profit-maximizing firm will employ additional physical capital until its MRP is equal to its cost, the interest rate that the firm must pay on the funds (financial capital) necessary to purchase the physical capital. At higher (lower) interest rates, firms will demand less (more) capital, both physical and financial.

> *Professor's Note: This concept is introduced here but is covered in more detail in the Corporate Finance topic review. Capital budgeting is the process of choosing only those firm investments for which the return on capital investment is greater than the firm's cost of investment funds.*

We need to add one additional point to account for an important difference between the MRP of capital and the MRP of labor. The additional output from employing an additional unit of labor is produced at the time that the labor is employed. With physical capital—a bulldozer, for example—the additional output will be produced over many periods into the future. For this reason, it is actually the present value of the future MRP of capital that will determine the return on a current investment in (physical) capital assets. In any event, the demand for financial capital will be a downward-sloping function of the interest rate (the cost of financial capital).

Professor's Note: We saw the concept of net present value of an investment in Quantitative Methods, and we will see examples of discounting the value of the future output of an asset to evaluate an investment opportunity in Corporate Finance.

Now that we have explained that the demand for financial capital is derived from the present value of MRP of physical capital in production, we can turn our attention to the **supply of financial capital**. Because the interest rate is the price of capital, the supply curve will be an upward-sloping function of interest rates. The suppliers of capital are savers, and they have the choice of consuming now or saving to consume later. Three primary factors influence savings and the supply of financial capital: interest rates, current incomes, and expected future incomes.

- At higher rates of interest, individuals are willing to save more because they will receive greater future amounts. Savers will save more (forego more consumption now) if they can consume 10% more next year than if they are only rewarded with 2% more consumption next year for foregoing consumption now.

- Increases in current income induce individuals to save more (increase the supply of capital), while decreases in current income have the opposite effect.

- If expected future incomes increase, individuals' willingness to trade current consumption for future consumption will decrease. Workers anticipating a decline in their incomes in retirement are motivated to save more now to smooth out their consumption over time. They will save more now (consume less) so that they can consume more in the future when their incomes are lower. College students are in the opposite situation and save little (or go into debt) in anticipation of rising incomes in the future. We can say that, in general, an increase (decrease) in expected future incomes will decrease (increase) the current supply of capital. Changes in current income and expected future income will shift the supply of capital curve; that is, at each interest rate, more or less capital will be supplied.

Equilibrium in the capital market determines interest rates. The interest rate where the quantity of capital supplied equals the quantity of capital demanded is the equilibrium (market) interest rate. Capital market equilibrium is illustrated in Figure 4.

Figure 4: Capital Market Equilibrium

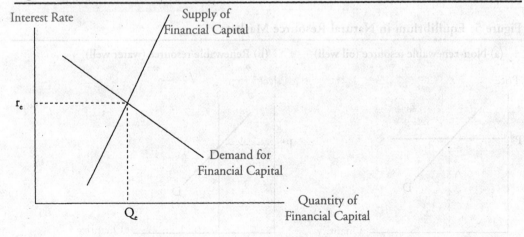

LOS 21.g: Differentiate between renewable and nonrenewable natural resources and describe the supply curve for each.

To understand the difference between the supply of **renewable and non-renewable resources**, assume you own two wells. One is an oil well and one is a water well. When you take a barrel of oil out of the oil well, it's gone forever—a non-renewable resource. When you take water out of the water well at a sustainable rate, it will be replaced by nature—a renewable resource.

Assuming a competitive market for water, the price will be determined by demand. The supply of renewable resources at a point in time, or per time period, is fixed. Land is also considered a renewable resource—using it now does not mean we cannot use it later, and its quantity is also fixed. The supply of a renewable resource is, therefore, independent of price and is perfectly inelastic.

The quantity of a non-renewable natural resource that has already been discovered is called the **known stock** of the resource. Though the known stock is fixed at any point in time, it tends to increase over time as technological advances make more resources accessible. The rate at which this resource is supplied, also called *flow supply*, is perfectly elastic at a price that equals the *present value* of the expected next-period price.

To understand this concept, assume that the price of oil is expected to rise at a rate greater than the risk-free interest rate. Oil-producing nations would curtail current production and produce more in the next period when the prices are expected to be higher. If the price of oil is expected to rise at a rate less than the risk-free interest rate, oil-producing nations are better off increasing their current production and investing the proceeds to earn the risk-free rate of return. Based on this principle (the Hotelling Principle), the equilibrium price of oil is expected to rise at a rate equal to the risk-free rate of interest.

Figure 5 illustrates, for a non-renewable resource, that the supply curve is perfectly elastic and the quantity supplied depends only on the demand at that price. For a renewable resource, supply is fixed (perfectly inelastic) and the price is determined by demand.

Figure 5: Equilibrium in Natural Resource Markets

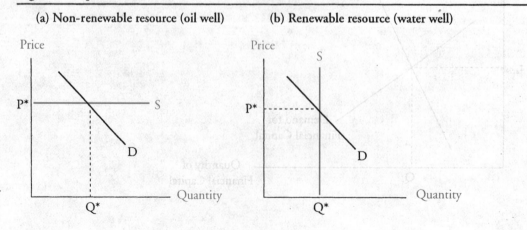

©2010 Kaplan, Inc.

LOS 21.h: Differentiate between economic rent and opportunity costs.

Differences in incomes are due to differences in workers' marginal revenue products. An actor who can star in a movie and fill theaters has a high marginal revenue product. A worker in a car wash has a low marginal revenue product.

The opportunity cost of an employee is what he could make in his next highest-paying alternative employment. For the worker in the car wash, this may be very close to the wage rate at the car wash. There are many opportunities for employment in low-skill/low marginal revenue product jobs.

The difference between what successful actors earn and what they could earn in their next highest-paying alternative may be quite large. This difference between a factor of production's earnings and opportunity cost is called **economic rent**. For many successful actors, a very large part of what they earn is economic rent.

Kelsey Grammer (star of a U.S. television show) earned $1.6 million per half-hour episode. Assuming that Grammer's opportunity cost for a week of work (his weekly earnings in his next highest-paying alternative occupation) was considerably less, he would have continued to be a television actor even if the weekly pay were considerably less than $1.6 million. We can think of the opportunity cost as the amount required to induce a person to do particular work or, alternatively, as the amount necessary to bid a factor of production away from its next highest-valued alternative use.

Economic rent is similar to the concept of producer's surplus and depends to a large extent on the shape of the supply curve for the resource. When the supply curve is perfectly elastic, as it is with a non-renewable resource, there is no economic rent. When the supply is perfectly inelastic, as it is with a renewable resource, the entire payment for the factor is economic rent. For an upward-sloping supply curve, economic rent is part of the total paid for the factor of production. These cases are illustrated in Figure 6.

If the factor of production is relatively easy to create or supply, economic rent is reduced by competition. If a factor of production is very difficult to supply or reproduce (like the skills of a professional athlete or musical performer), *and the factor has a high marginal revenue product*, the factor will receive significant economic rent. Scarcity is not enough. The skill of a top-flight curling player may be in very short supply, but they do not receive anywhere near the rent that a soccer star does.

Figure 6: Economic Rent to Factors of Production

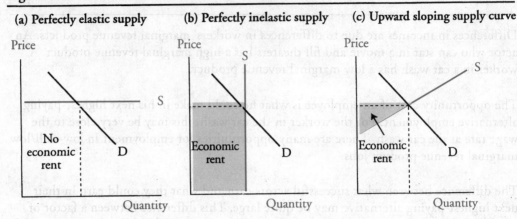

KEY CONCEPTS

LOS 21.a

Demand for productive resources is derived from the demand for the consumer goods they are used to produce.

Marginal revenue is the addition to total revenue from selling the next unit of output. Marginal revenue product (MRP) is the addition to total revenue from selling the additional output that results from using one more unit of a productive resource (input), holding the quantities of other inputs constant.

The MRP of labor determines the wage rate because employers maximize profits by adding units of labor as long as the MRP of the next unit is greater than the wage rate.

LOS 21.b

An increase in product price, an increase in the price of a substitute resource, and a decrease in the price of a complementary resource will all increase the demand for labor (or any productive resource in general).

The elasticity of demand for labor will be greater the longer the adjustment period, the greater the proportion of labor in the production process, and the greater degree to which other factors of production (capital) can be substituted for labor.

LOS 21.c

The supply of labor increases with the wage rate because of the substitution effect (workers substitute labor hours for leisure hours), but is limited by the income effect (workers' demand for leisure increases as their income increases).

The size of the adult population and the accumulation of capital in items that allow more adults to work outside the home are factors that bring about changes in the supply of labor.

LOS 21.d

Labor unions bargain for workers as a group and attempt to restrict supply in order to increase the wage rate for union members. Unions also attempt to increase the demand for their members' labor by (1) instituting training programs for union members to increase their productivity, (2) encouraging the purchase of union-made goods or domestically manufactured goods in general, (3) getting import restrictions enacted for goods that compete with those produced by union workers, (4) limiting the supply of immigrant labor, and (5) increasing the minimum wage for unskilled workers (a substitute for union workers).

A monopsonist employer will hire additional workers only until the marginal cost of an additional worker is equal to the worker's MRP, resulting in a less-than-efficient quantity of labor demanded and output of the final good or service.

LOS 21.e

As a firm's demand for physical capital (machinery and other productive physical assets) to expand production increases, so does its demand for financial capital (the funds necessary to purchase physical capital).

LOS 21.f

A firm will invest in more physical capital when the returns, based on the present value of the future marginal revenue product of additional physical capital, are greater than the cost of the financial capital required to purchase additional physical capital.

The equilibrium interest rate in the market for financial capital is determined by the demand for financial capital for funding investment by businesses, and the supply of capital by savers, which depends primarily on interest rates, current incomes, and expected future incomes.

LOS 21.g

Theoretical models suggest that for non-renewable natural resources, supply is perfectly elastic at the present value of the expected future price, while for renewable natural resources, supply is perfectly inelastic at the sustainable quantity of production.

LOS 21.h

An employee's opportunity cost of employment is the amount the employee could earn in his next-highest valued alternative employment. Economic rent is the amount by which a person's earnings exceed his opportunity cost. People who have scarce skills and a relatively high marginal revenue product can earn significant economic rent.

CONCEPT CHECKERS

1. The marginal revenue product is *best* defined as the:
    A. addition to total revenue from selling one more unit of output.
    B. additional output produced by using one more unit of a productive input.
    C. gain in revenue from selling the output produced by using one more unit of an input.

2. For a firm that holds all other resource inputs constant, a curve depicting the marginal revenue product of a resource will be:
    A. identical to the firm's supply curve of the final product.
    B. identical to the firm's demand curve for the resource.
    C. the mirror image of the firm's supply curve of the final product.

3. In a given firm, skilled workers currently produce twice as much of its product as unskilled workers do per hour worked. Skilled workers earn $20 per hour, and unskilled workers earn $8 per hour. Based on this information, the firm should:
    A. increase the use of skilled workers and/or decrease the use of unskilled workers.
    B. increase the use of unskilled workers and/or decrease the use of skilled workers.
    C. increase the salary of skilled workers to attract more of them.

4. Which of the following is *most likely* to cause an increase in the demand for labor?
    A. An increase in the demand for final goods or services.
    B. A decrease in the price of substitute technologies.
    C. A decrease in the productivity of labor.

5. Which of the following will be *most likely* to cause a decrease in the demand for a specific type of labor?
    A. A decrease in the number of workers who specialize in that type of labor.
    B. A decrease in the prices of machines that are substitutes in production for that type of labor.
    C. An increase in the productivity of workers who specialize in doing that type of labor.

6. If firms decide to increase their production capacity, what is the *most likely* effect on the demand for physical and financial capital?
    A. Both will increase.
    B. Both will decrease.
    C. One will increase and one will decrease.

7. A firm will employ physical capital up to the level where the present value of the marginal revenue product of capital is equal to the:
    A. wage rate.
    B. firm's cost of capital.
    C. marginal revenue product of labor.

8. The supply of financial capital is *least likely* to be influenced by which of the
    following?
    A. Interest rates.
    B. MRP of physical capital.
    C. Consumers' incomes.

9. The supply of a renewable resource is:
    A. the known stock.
    B. perfectly elastic.
    C. perfectly inelastic.

10. The difference between what a worker earns and what she could earn from her
    next best alternative employment is called:
    A. economic rent.
    B. opportunity cost.
    C. marginal revenue product.

11. A union would *least likely* increase the demand for its members' labor by:
    A. collective bargaining with the employer.
    B. political activism supporting the enactment of more restrictive immigration
        laws.
    C. advertisements encouraging consumers to purchase union-made goods.

ANSWERS – CONCEPT CHECKERS

1. **C** The marginal revenue product is the addition to total revenue gained by selling the marginal product (additional output) from employing one more unit of a productive resource.

2. **B** This is true because the firm will maximize profits in this case by employing the variable resource until price equals marginal revenue product. As it increases the use of the resource, marginal revenue product falls. The negative relationship between quantity used and marginal revenue product is identical to the relationship between quantity demanded and price.

3. **B** The firm should try to equate hourly output with hourly wage for both types of workers. As it is, that ratio is higher for unskilled workers. The firm should substitute away from skilled workers toward unskilled workers. To maximize profits, wage must equal a worker's MRP; skilled workers should not have more than twice the wage of unskilled workers when their MRP is only twice as much.

4. **A** The demand for labor is a derived demand. When the demand for the final good or service increases, the price of that final good or service increases, which increases the MRP (and demand) for labor.

5. **B** If the prices of substitutes for a specific type of labor fall, the firm will substitute away from that type of labor. This means the demand for that type of labor will decrease.

6. **A** If firms are increasing their production capacity, they need to acquire equipment, so the demand for physical capital increases. To buy that equipment, they need to raise funds, so the demand for financial capital increases. The greater the demand for physical capital, the greater the demand for the financial capital (money raised through issuing securities) necessary to purchase the physical capital.

7. **B** A profit-maximizing firm will equate the present value of the $MRP_{Capital}$ to the cost of capital.

8. **B** The MRP of physical capital determines the demand for financial capital. Interest rates and consumers' current and expected incomes are the primary factors that determine the supply of financial capital.

9. **C** For a renewable resource, supply is independent of price and is therefore perfectly inelastic. Known stock is the quantity of a non-renewable resource that has been discovered.

10. **A** Economic rent is what a worker earns above what she could earn from her next best alternative employment. Opportunity cost is what she could earn from her next best alternative employment.

11. **A** Collective bargaining usually is aimed at restricting supply rather than influencing demand. Restricting immigration reduces the supply of a substitute (unskilled immigrant labor) and thus increases the demand for union labor. Because labor demand is derived from demand for the final good or service, increasing the demand for the union-made good or service will tend to increase the demand for union labor.

The following is a review of the Economics principles designed to address the learning outcome statements set forth by CFA Institute®. This topic is also covered in:

MONITORING JOBS AND THE PRICE LEVEL

EXAM FOCUS

The level of unemployment and the rate of inflation are two very important considerations in evaluating the performance of the economy and in determining the course of monetary and fiscal policy. You should learn the terminology related to employment statistics and be able to distinguish among the three sources of unemployment. The concepts of the natural rate of unemployment and full employment are quite important in evaluating economic performance. Finally, you should understand how the consumer price index (CPI) is calculated, because it is not simply a measure of general price inflation but is important in economic policy decisions. The CPI determines adjustments to wages in many union contracts, Social Security retirement benefit payments, and the returns on some securities issued by the U.S. Treasury. Many believe that the method of calculating the CPI results in an upward bias of approximately 1% per year in the estimated rate of inflation.

LOS 22.a: Define an unemployed person and interpret the main labor market indicators.

A person who is not working is considered to be an **unemployed person** if he is available to work and:

- has actively searched for work in the last four weeks, or
- has been laid off from a job and is waiting to be recalled, or
- will start a new job in the next 30 days.

The **unemployment rate** is the percentage of people in the labor force who are unemployed. The **labor force** includes all people who are either employed or actively seeking employment.

$$\text{unemployment rate} = \frac{\text{number of unemployed}}{\text{labor force}} \times 100$$

The unemployment rate decreases during expansions and increases during recessions.

The **labor-force participation rate** is the percentage of the working-age population who are either employed or actively seeking employment. The **working-age population** is all people 16 years of age or older who are not living in institutions.

$$\text{labor-force participation rate} = \frac{\text{labor force}}{\text{working-age population}} \times 100$$

©2010 Kaplan, Inc.

Short-term fluctuations in the labor-force participation rate can occur because of changes in the number of **discouraged workers**, those who are available for work but are neither employed nor actively seeking employment. The labor force participation rate tends to increase when the economy expands and decrease during recessions. Discouraged workers who stopped seeking jobs during a recession are motivated to seek work again once the expansion takes hold and they believe their prospects of finding work are better.

The **employment-to-population ratio** is the percentage of the working-age population who are employed.

$$\text{employment-to-population ratio} = \frac{\text{number of employed}}{\text{working-age population}} \times 100$$

The employment-to-population ratio tends to increase during expansions (when unemployment is low) and decrease during recessions (when unemployment is high).

LOS 22.b: Define aggregate hours and real wage rates and explain their relation to gross domestic product (GDP).

The employment indicators we have discussed so far reflect the number of people who have jobs, but to know how much total labor is being performed, we also need to consider how much time workers are working on average. To capture the effects of part-time work and overtime, we measure **aggregate hours**, the total number of hours worked in a year by all employed people.

Aggregate hours have shown a long-term upward trend, but they have not grown as fast as the labor force because the *average workweek* (weekly hours worked per person) has been declining over time. Both aggregate hours and the workweek tend to increase during expansions and decrease during recessions.

Aggregate hours worked is an important measure because it allows us to estimate the *productivity* of labor, the amount of output produced per hour worked. The more productive an hour of labor is, the higher *wage rate* labor can receive. **Real wage rates** are money wage rates adjusted for changes in the overall price level. Real wage rates tell us what an hour's labor is paid in terms of goods and services.

Real wage rates tend to fluctuate with the productivity of labor and are calculated using *total labor compensation,* which includes wages, salaries, and employer-paid benefits.

LOS 22.c: Explain the types of unemployment, full employment, the natural rate of unemployment, and the relation between unemployment and real GDP.

There are three types of unemployment:

1. **Frictional unemployment** results from constant changes in the economy that prevent *qualified* workers from being matched with existing job openings in a timely manner. Employees spend time and effort seeking work, and employers spend time and effort

seeking workers. Unemployment resulting from this job search activity, referred to as frictional unemployment, is always with us as employers expand or contract their businesses and workers move, are fired, or quit to seek other opportunities.

2. **Structural unemployment** is caused by (structural) changes in the economy that eliminate some jobs while generating others for which unemployed workers are not qualified. Structural unemployment differs from frictional unemployment in that the unemployed workers do not currently have the skills needed to perform the newly created jobs.

3. **Cyclical unemployment** is caused by changes in the general level of economic output. When the economy is operating at less than full capacity, cyclical unemployment is present.

Full employment is the condition that exists when the economy has no cyclical unemployment. Note, however, that both structural and frictional unemployment continue to exist even when the economy is at full employment. In other words, some level of unemployment is expected when the economy is at full employment. The sum of the frictional and structural unemployment rates is called the **natural rate of unemployment**.

Potential GDP is the (theoretical) level of output the economy can produce when unemployment is at the natural rate. When real GDP falls below potential GDP, cyclical unemployment increases. When real GDP rises toward and beyond potential GDP, cyclical unemployment decreases. Economists have a range of opinions about what the natural rate of unemployment really is, so estimates of potential GDP and cyclical unemployment will differ.

LOS 22.d: Explain and calculate the consumer price index (CPI) and the inflation rate, describe the relation between the CPI and the inflation rate, and explain the main sources of CPI bias.

The **consumer price index** (CPI) is the best known indicator of U.S. inflation. The CPI measures the average price for a defined basket of goods and services that represents the purchasing patterns of a typical urban household. The Bureau of Labor Statistics (BLS) reports the CPI monthly.

The BLS constructs the CPI in three stages:

1. **Select the CPI basket.** The first step is to determine what goods and services a typical household buys. The BLS surveys a large sample of consumers to determine what percentage of their income consumers spend on which items. These percentages become the weights for each of the more than 80,000 goods in the overall index. The current weights for the eight major categories in the CPI are shown in Figure 1.

Figure 1: Relative Importance in the CPI as of December 2009*

Category	Percent of Index
Housing	42.0%
Transportation	16.7%
Food and beverages	14.8%
Medical care	6.5%
Education and communication	6.4%
Recreation	6.4%
Apparel	3.7%
Other goods and services	3.5%

*Source: Bureau of Labor Statistics, U.S. Department of Labor

2. **Conduct a monthly price survey.** Every month, the BLS records the prices of every item in the CPI in 30 urban areas. The surveyors also record any changes in the individual products, such as package sizes, and adjust prices to make them comparable to past prices.

3. **Calculate the CPI.** This calculation is done in three steps.

Step 1: Find the cost of the CPI basket for the **reference base period**.
Step 2: Find the cost of the CPI basket for the **current period**.
Step 3: Calculate the CPI for both periods. The formula for the index is:

$$CPI = \frac{\text{cost of basket at current prices}}{\text{cost of basket at base period prices}} \times 100$$

Example: Calculating a consumer price index

The following table shows price information for a simplified basket of goods. Calculate a CPI for this basket in the current period.

Item	Quantity	Price in Base Period	Current Price
Cheeseburgers	200	2.50	3.00
Movie tickets	50	7.00	10.00
Gasoline, gallons	300	1.50	3.00
Digital watches	100	12.00	9.00

Answer:

Reference base period:

Cheeseburgers	200 × 2.50	=	500
Movie tickets	50 × 7.00	=	350
Gasoline	300 × 1.50	=	450
Watches	100 × 12.00	=	1,200
Cost of CPI basket			2,500

Current period:

Cheeseburgers	200 × 3.00	=	600
Movie tickets	50 × 10.00	=	500
Gasoline	300 × 3.00	=	900
Watches	100 × 9.00	=	900
Cost of CPI basket			2,900

$$\text{CPI}_{current} = \frac{\text{cost of basket in current period}}{\text{cost of basket in base period}} \times 100$$

$$\text{CPI}_{current} = \frac{2,900}{2,500} \times 100 = 116$$

The **inflation rate** is the percentage change in the price level from a year ago. The CPI is one of the primary indicators used to measure the inflation rate. As measured by the CPI, the inflation rate is given by the following formula:

$$\text{inflation rate} = \frac{\text{current CPI} - \text{year-ago CPI}}{\text{year-ago CPI}} \times 100$$

Example: Calculating the inflation rate based on CPI

The CPI for all items was 202.9 in June 2006 and 194.5 in June 2005. The CPI for all items less energy was 203.6 in June 2006 and 198.5 in June 2005. Calculate and interpret the inflation rate based on these two measures.

Answer:

$$\text{all items: } \frac{202.9 - 194.5}{194.5} \times 100 = 4.3\%$$

$$\text{all items ex-energy: } \frac{203.6 - 198.5}{198.5} \times 100 = 2.6\%$$

As measured by the CPI, the inflation rate for goods excluding energy was less than the inflation rate for all items over this 12-month period. This means energy prices must have been increasing faster than the overall price level.

Example: Using the CPI to calculate real price changes

In 1980, the average gasoline price in the United States was $1.23/gallon, and in 2006 it was $2.60/gallon. The urban consumer price index (1967 = 100) was 246.8 in 1980 and 603.9 in 2006. What was the change in real gasoline prices over the period?

Answer:

We can use the CPI to convert the 2006 price to a 1980 equivalent price, or to convert the 1980 price to its 2006 equivalent, to calculate the real price change.

convert to 1980 price: $2.60\left(\dfrac{246.8}{603.9}\right) = \$1.063$

So the real price of gas declined by $\dfrac{1.063}{1.23} - 1 = -13.6\%$

convert to 2006 price : $1.23\left(\dfrac{603.9}{246.8}\right) = \$3.01$

Again, the real price decline was $\dfrac{2.60}{3.01} - 1 = -13.6\%$

While average gas prices increased $\dfrac{2.60}{1.23} - 1 = 111\%$, the CPI increased

$\dfrac{603.9}{246.8} - 1 = 144.7\%$, so the inflation adjusted gasoline price actually declined over the period.

CPI Bias

The CPI is widely believed to overstate the true rate of inflation. The price data the BLS collects reflect long-term structural shifts that should not be included in a measure of the price level. The most significant biases in the CPI data include:

- **New goods.** Older products are often replaced by newer but initially more expensive products. This biases the index because some newly available goods perform the same function as different lower-priced goods in the base-period market basket.
- **Quality changes.** If the price of a product increases because the product has improved, the price increase is not due to inflation but still causes an increase in the price index.
- **Commodity substitution.** Even in an inflation-free economy, prices of goods relative to each other change all the time. When two goods are substitutes for each other, consumers increase their purchases of the relatively cheaper good and buy less of the relatively more expensive good. Over time, such changes can make the CPI's fixed basket of goods a less accurate measure of typical household spending.
- **Outlet substitution.** When consumers shift their purchases toward discount outlets and away from convenience outlets, they reduce their cost of living in a way the CPI does not capture.

Estimates are that the CPI overstates inflation by about 1% per year. This upward bias in the CPI distorts economic decisions. Many employment contracts with cost-of-living adjustments are based on the rate of increase in the CPI. A substantial portion of government spending, such as entitlement payments, increases automatically with the CPI. The BLS is attempting to reduce the bias by surveying consumers more frequently and re-evaluating the weighting method.

KEY CONCEPTS

LOS 22.a

A person who is available for work is considered unemployed if he is actively seeking work, waiting to be called back to a job, or waiting for the start date of a new job.

The main labor market indicators include the unemployment rate, the labor force participation rate, and the employment-to-population ratio.

$$\text{unemployment rate} = \frac{\text{number of unemployed}}{\text{labor force}} \times 100$$

$$\text{labor-force participation rate} = \frac{\text{labor force}}{\text{working-age population}} \times 100$$

$$\text{employment-to-population ratio} = \frac{\text{number of employed}}{\text{working-age population}} \times 100$$

LOS 22.b

Aggregate hours are the total number of hours worked in a year by all employed people. Real wage rates are money wage rates adjusted for changes in the price level.

Increases in aggregate hours worked and the real wage rate, which is primarily determined by labor productivity, both lead to increases in real GDP and economic expansion.

LOS 22.c

Frictional unemployment results from the time it takes for employers and employees to find each other. Structural unemployment results from long-term economic changes that require workers to gain new skills to fill new jobs. Cyclical unemployment exists when the economy is producing less than its potential output.

Full employment refers to a situation where the economy has reached its potential level of GDP because cyclical unemployment is zero, although both frictional and structural unemployment are always present. The sum of the rates of frictional and structural unemployment is called the natural rate of unemployment.

LOS 22.d

The consumer price index (CPI) is a measure of the average prices of goods and services designed to represent the purchases of a typical urban household.

The inflation rate is measured as the annual percentage change in the CPI.

$$\text{inflation percent rate} = \frac{\text{current CPI} - \text{year-ago CPI}}{\text{year-ago CPI}} \times 100$$

Because of biases that arise from new goods, quality improvements, and consumers' decisions to make substitutions among goods and seek lower-priced shopping outlets, the CPI is believed to overstate the true rate of inflation by about 1% per year.

CONCEPT CHECKERS

1. The unemployment rate is defined as the number of unemployed as a percentage of the:
   A. labor force.
   B. working-age population.
   C. civilian noninstitutional population.

2. Which of the following indicators moves inversely with the business cycle?
   A. Unemployment rate.
   B. Labor force participation rate.
   C. Employment-to-population ratio.

3. Which measure of the labor market includes discouraged workers?
   A. Labor force.
   B. Working-age population.
   C. Number of unemployed.

4. Which of the following would be counted as frictional unemployment?
   A. Due to the negative growth of GDP, Smith was laid off.
   B. Johnson was fired from his job after he got into an argument with his foreman and has not sought a new job.
   C. Although there were jobs available, Jones was unable to find an employer with a satisfactory opening.

5. Which of the following would be counted as structural unemployment?
   A. Due to the negative growth of GDP, Smith was laid off.
   B. Although there were jobs available, Johnson was unable to find an employer with a satisfactory opening.
   C. When the plant was modernized, Jones lost her job because she did not have the skill needed to operate the new equipment.

6. Given the following hypothetical information about the conditions in the labor market:

Employed	177,000
Discouraged workers	2,000
Unemployed	13,000
Household workers	20,000
Students	15,000
Retirees	19,000
Disabled	5,000
Labor force	190,000
Civilian population 16 and over	249,000

   What is the unemployment rate?
   A. 5.3%.
   B. 6.8%.
   C. 7.9%.

7.   The value of an hour's labor in terms of goods and services is called:
      A. the real wage rate.
      B. the nominal wage rate.
      C. total labor compensation.

Use the following table to answer Questions 8 to 10.

CPI data for a recent 12-month period:

Category	Percent of Index	Current Level	Year-ago Level
Commodities	40.0	160	151
Services	60.0	230	223
All items	100.0	?	?

8.   The current level of the CPI for all items is *closest* to:
      A. 194.
      B. 202.
      C. 390.

9.   The annual inflation rate as measured by CPI was *closest* to:
      A. 3%.
      B. 4%.
      C. 5%.

10.   Given the bias that is generally believed to exist in the CPI, the true rate of
      inflation was *most likely*:
      A. 3%.
      B. 4%.
      C. 5%.

ANSWERS – CONCEPT CHECKERS

1. **A** The unemployment rate is the number of unemployed as a percentage of the labor force.

2. **A** The unemployment rate increases when GDP decreases, and decreases when GDP increases. The other indicators move in the same direction as the business cycle.

3. **B** Discouraged workers are not employed and not seeking employment and are therefore not counted as part of the labor force or among the unemployed. They are, however, included in the working-age population.

4. **C** One of the causes of frictional unemployment is that information regarding prospective employees and employers is costly and sometimes hard to find. The other cause of frictional unemployment is that both employees and employers may spend some time looking for information that will match them up.

5. **C** Structural unemployment exists when changes in the economy eliminate some jobs while generating new job openings for which unemployed workers are not qualified.

6. **B** Unemployment rate = (number of unemployed) / (number in the labor force). In this question, household workers, students, retirees, and the disabled are not considered unemployed. Thus, the unemployment rate is calculated as: (13,000) / (190,000) = 6.8%.

7. **A** The real wage rate measures the purchasing power of an hour's labor. The nominal wage rate is the money value of an hour's labor. Productivity is output per hour of labor, one of the determinants of the real wage rate. Total labor compensation is one of the measures of the real wage rate.

8. **B** $0.4(160) + 0.6(230) = 202.0$

9. **B** current index level = 202.0 (from Question 8)

   year-ago index level = $0.4(151) + 0.6(223) = 194.2$

   inflation rate = $\dfrac{202.0 - 194.2}{194.2} \times 100 = 4.0\%$

10. **A** The CPI calculation is generally believed to add about 1% to the actual inflation rate.

The following is a review of the Economics principles designed to address the learning outcome statements set forth by CFA Institute®. This topic is also covered in:

Aggregate Supply and Aggregate Demand

Exam Focus

The title says it all, but you should spend some quality time here getting the details down. This is the model of equilibrium output and price level for the overall economy, and it is used repeatedly for analysis in the topic reviews that follow. Learn it well; no breaks here. Learn the differences between the classical, Keynesian, and monetarist views of economic equilibrium and growth too.

LOS 23.a: Explain the factors that influence real GDP and long-run and short-run aggregate supply, explain movement along the long-run and short-run aggregate supply curves (LAS and SAS), and discuss the reasons for changes in potential GDP and aggregate supply.

Aggregate supply refers to the amount of goods and services produced by an economy. Aggregate supply is a function of the price level. Just as in goods markets, higher prices bring about a greater amount of supply in the short run. Figure 1 illustrates a short-run aggregate supply (SAS) curve and a long-run aggregate supply (LAS) curve. The overall price level in the economy is on the vertical axis and the real level of output of goods and services (real GDP) is on the horizontal axis.

Figure 1: Aggregate Supply in the Long Run and Short Run

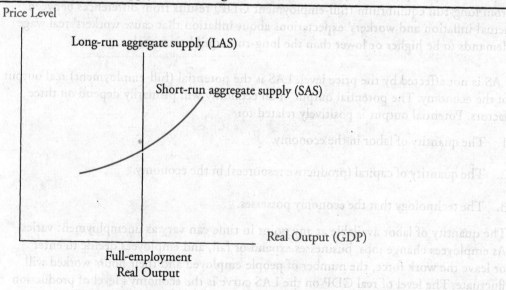

©2010 Kaplan, Inc.

First we will address the questions of why the LAS curve is a vertical line and why the SAS curve is upward-sloping. Then we will discuss the factors that cause the curves to shift over time.

Recall that in our discussion of microeconomic principles we defined the *short run* as that period of time for which the quantities of some productive inputs were fixed and the *long run* as a period of time over which all factors of production, including plant size, could be adjusted. The short run and long run in our aggregate supply and demand model are defined differently. While a bit of a simplification, you can generally take the **short run in the aggregate demand and supply model** to be that period over which workers' wage demands are constant. We say that the short-run aggregate supply curve is constructed holding the money wage (not the real wage) constant.

A key factor that drives workers' wage demands in this model is their expectations about future rates of inflation. An increase in workers' expectations about future inflation increases their wage demands, and this decreases short-run aggregate supply. Higher real wage costs (money wages up at each price level) increase the marginal costs of production, and employers will produce less at each price level when wages are higher.

Long-run aggregate supply represents the supply of goods and services at each price level when workers' inflation expectations are just equal to actual inflation. Therefore, an increase in the actual rate of inflation that does not change workers' inflation expectations does not shift the short-run aggregate supply curve (SAS). A change in actual inflation, holding workers' money wage demands constant, leads to movement along the SAS curve to a temporary disequilibrium situation, either above or below full-employment GDP (LRAS).

We assume that in the long run, expected inflation must equal actual inflation, and this leads to economic production at full-employment GDP, that is, with no cyclical unemployment. As workers' inflation expectations adjust and equal actual inflation, the SAS curve shifts in a way that returns us to equilibrium at full-employment real GDP. It will be very helpful to keep this relation in mind, as in this model any deviation from long-run equilibrium (full-employment GDP) results from differences between actual inflation and workers' expectations about inflation that cause workers' real wage demands to be higher or lower than the long-run equilibrium real wage rate.

LAS is not affected by the price level. LAS is the potential (full-employment) real output of the economy. The potential output of an economy will primarily depend on three factors. Potential output is positively related to:

1. The quantity of labor in the economy.

2. The quantity of capital (productive resources) in the economy.

3. The technology that the economy possesses.

The quantity of labor available at any point in time can vary as unemployment varies. As employees change jobs, businesses expand or fail, and employees decide to enter or leave the work force, the number of people employed and their hours worked will fluctuate. The level of real GDP on the LAS curve is the economy's level of production when the economy is operating at full employment. Full employment does not mean zero unemployment. There will always be some unemployment as workers search for the best available job, employers search for the best available employee, and changes in the economy leave workers from industries with decreasing employment without the necessary skills to work in expanding industries. There is a natural rate of unemployment corresponding to the level of real GDP along the LAS curve. That level of output is referred to as full-employment GDP. As we will see, the economy can operate at less than full-employment GDP during a recession when cyclical unemployment is high, and (temporarily) at above full-employment GDP during periods of rapid economic growth.

Over time, the LAS curve may shift as the full-employment quantity of labor changes, as the amount of available capital in the economy changes, or as technology improves the productivity of capital, labor, or both.

In the short run, firms will respond to changes in the prices of goods and services. The key to understanding movements *along* the SAS curve is to understand that we are allowing the prices of final goods and services to vary, while holding the wage rate and the price of other productive resources constant in the short run. When goods and services prices rise (fall), businesses have an incentive to expand (reduce) production, and real GDP will increase (decrease) above (below) the full-employment level shown by the LAS curve. This is why we show real GDP as an upward sloping function of the price level along the SAS curve. Again, in the macroeconomic short run, we are holding the money wage rate, other resource prices, and potential GDP (LAS) constant.

Next, we turn our attention to the factors that will shift the SAS curve. Our list begins with those factors that also shift the LAS curve. The SAS and LAS curves will both shift when the full-employment quantity of labor changes, the amount of available capital in the economy changes, or as technology improves the productivity capital, labor, or both.

In Figure 2, we illustrate the effects on LAS and SAS that would result from an increase in full-employment GDP, due to an increase in labor, capital, or an advance in technology. Long-run aggregate supply increases to LAS$_2$ and short-run aggregate supply increases to SAS$_2$.

Figure 2: An Increase in Potential GDP

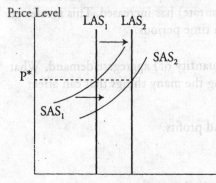

There are some factors that will shift SAS but not affect LAS. We held the money wage rate and other resource prices constant in constructing the SAS curve. If the wage rate or prices of other productive inputs increase, the SAS curve will shift to the left, a decrease in short-run aggregate supply. When businesses observe a rise in resource prices, they will decrease their output as the profit maximizing level of output declines.

Two important factors influence the change in money wage rates. One is unemployment; when unemployment rises, it puts downward pressure on the money wage rate as there is an excess supply of labor at the current rate. Conversely, if the economy is temporarily operating above full-employment levels, there will be upward pressure on the money wage rate. The second factor that can influence the money wage rate is inflation expectations. An expected increase in inflation will lead to increases in the money wage rate and an expected decrease in inflation will slow the increase of money wages.

LOS 23.b: Explain the components of and the factors that affect real GDP demanded, describe the aggregate demand curve and why it slopes downward, and explain the factors that can change aggregate demand.

We turn our attention now to the **aggregate demand** curve. The aggregate demand curve shows the relation between the price level and the real quantity of final goods and services (real GDP) demanded. The components of aggregate demand are:

- Consumption (C).
- Investment (I).
- Government spending (G).
- Net exports (X), which is exports minus imports.

aggregate demand = C + I + G + X

The aggregate demand curve is downward-sloping (a good thing for a demand curve!) because at higher price levels, consumption, business investment, and exports will all likely decrease. There are two effects here to consider. First, when the price level rises, individuals' real wealth decreases. Since they have less accumulated wealth in real terms, individuals will spend less. This is referred to as the *wealth effect*. Second, when the price level increases, interest rates will rise. An increase in interest rates decreases business investment (I) as well as consumption (C) as consumers delay or forego purchases of consumer durables such as cars, appliances, and home repairs. This is a substitution effect, as consumers substitute consumption later for consumption now because the cost of consuming goods now instead of later (the interest rate) has increased. This is referred to as *intertemporal substitution*, substitution between time periods.

So changes in the price level cause changes in (the quantity of) aggregate demand. What factors will shift the aggregate demand curve? Among the many things that can affect aggregate demand there are three primary factors:

- Expectations about future incomes, inflation, and profits.
- Fiscal and monetary policy.
- World economy.

An increase in expected inflation will increase aggregate demand as consumers accelerate purchases to avoid higher prices in the future. An expectation of higher incomes in the future also will cause consumers to increase purchases in anticipation of these higher incomes. An increase in expected profits will lead businesses to increase their investment in plant and equipment.

©2010 Kaplan, Inc.

Fiscal policy refers to government policy with regard to spending, taxes, and transfer payments. An increase in spending increases the government component (G) of aggregate demand. A decrease in taxes or an increase in transfer payments (e.g., social security benefits or unemployment compensation) will increase the amount that consumers have to spend (their disposable income) and increase aggregate demand through an increase in consumption (C).

Monetary policy refers to the central bank's decisions to increase or decrease the money supply. An increase in the money supply will tend to decrease interest rates and increase consumption and investment spending, increasing aggregate demand. We will look at both monetary and fiscal policy effects more closely in subsequent topic reviews.

The state of the world economy will influence a country's aggregate demand through the net exports (X) component. If foreign incomes increase, foreign demand for the country's exports will increase, increasing X. If the country's foreign exchange rate increases (foreign currency buys fewer domestic currency units), its goods are relatively more expensive to foreigners, and exports will decrease. At the same time, imports will be relatively cheaper and the quantity of imported goods demanded will increase. Both effects will tend to decrease net exports (exports minus imports, X) and consequently decrease aggregate demand. A decrease in a country's exchange rate (currency depreciation) will have the opposite effect, increasing exports, decreasing imports, and increasing net exports and aggregate demand.

LOS 23.c: Differentiate between short-run and long-run macroeconomic equilibrium and explain how economic growth, inflation, and changes in aggregate demand and supply influence the macroeconomic equilibrium.

Now we examine **macroeconomic equilibrium** in the short run and in the long run.

In Figure 3, we illustrate long-run equilibrium at the intersection of the LAS curve and the aggregate demand curve. Just as we saw that price was the variable that led us to equilibrium in the goods market in microeconomics, here changes in the price level of final goods and services can move the economy to long-run macroeconomic equilibrium. In Figure 3, equilibrium is at a price level of 110. If we are at a short-run disequilibrium with the price level at 115, there is excess supply; the quantity of real goods and services supplied exceeds the (aggregate) demand for real goods and services. This is sometimes termed a recessionary gap, and there will be downward pressure on prices. Businesses will see a build-up of inventories and will decrease both production and prices in response. This will result in a decrease in the price level, which will move the economy toward long-run equilibrium at a price level of 110. If the price level were 105, there would be excess demand for real goods and services. This is sometimes referred to as an **inflationary gap**. Businesses will experience unintended decreases in inventories and respond by increasing output and prices. As the price level increases, the economy moves along the aggregate demand curve toward long-run equilibrium.

Figure 3: Long-Run Equilibrium Real Output

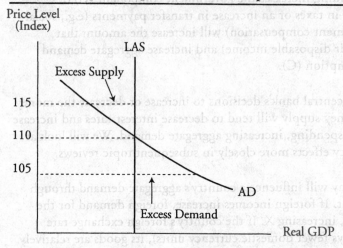

We will now extend this analysis to include shifts in short-run aggregate supply that are part of the process of moving toward the long-run equilibrium output and price level. Recall that in constructing the SAS curve we held money wages and other resource prices constant. If the economy is in short-run equilibrium, but at a level of output above or below full-employment GDP, it is in long-run disequilibrium. In Figure 4, we illustrate two situations where the economy is in short-run equilibrium but not in long-run equilibrium. In panel (a), short-run equilibrium real GDP, GDP_1, is less than full-employment GDP (along the LAS curve) and we would interpret this as a recession, or below full-employment equilibrium. This difference between real GDP and full-employment GDP is called a **recessionary gap** or **output gap**. As we will detail, this brings downward pressure on money wages and resource prices that will decrease the equilibrium price level from P_1 to P^*.

The opposite situation, above full-employment equilibrium, is illustrated in panel (b), where the short-run equilibrium real GDP, GDP_1, is above the full-employment level. This would be the situation in an economic expansion where aggregate demand has grown faster than LAS. The result will be upward pressure on prices that will result in inflation as the general price level increases from P_1 to P^*.

Figure 4: Long-Run Disequilibrium

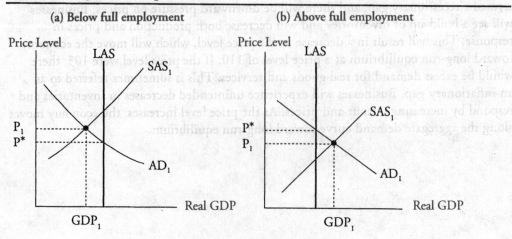

We have essentially described the phases of a business cycle here as deviations of short-run equilibrium real GDP below full-employment GDP (recession) and above full-employment GDP (expansion leading to inflationary pressure). How does this happen? Changes in aggregate demand can drive these business cycles.

Consider the short-run and long-run adjustment to an increase in aggregate demand illustrated in Figure 5. From an initial state of long-run equilibrium at the intersection of AD_0 with LAS, assume that aggregate demand increases to AD_1. The new short-run equilibrium will be at over-full employment with real GDP, GDP_1, above full-employment GDP, GDP*. The increase in the price level (from P_0 to P_{SR}) at the new equilibrium level means that workers' real wages have decreased (we are holding money wages constant in the short run). At the same time, the increase in demand will cause businesses to attempt to increase production, which will require hiring more workers. These two factors both lead to increased money wage demands. As these demands are met, we get a shift in the SAS curve from SAS_0 to SAS_1, which will restore long-run macroeconomic equilibrium at full-employment real GDP and at a new price level of P_{LR}. Note that an increase in the money wage and other *resource* prices means that business will be willing to supply less real goods and services at each price level (prices of final goods and services). It is the increase in resource prices that causes SAS to decrease.

Figure 5: Adjustment to an Increase in Aggregate Demand

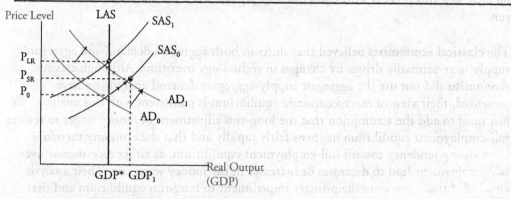

In Figure 6, we illustrate how a decrease in aggregate demand from AD_0 to AD_1 will lead to a new short-run equilibrium with the price level at P_{SR} and real GDP at GDP_1. GDP_1 is less than full-employment GDP (a recession). The resulting excess supply of labor (workers seeking jobs) will put downward pressure on money wage rates and other resource prices. This will lead to a shift in SAS to SAS_1 (an increase in supply), restoring long-run equilibrium at full-employment GDP along the LAS curve and at a new, lower price level of P_{LR}. Remember, a decrease in wages and other input prices increases short-run aggregate supply.

Figure 6: Adjustment to a Decrease in Aggregate Demand

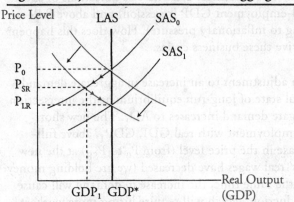

LOS 23.d: Compare and contrast the classical, Keynesian, and monetarist schools of macroeconomics.

While our discussion of the forces leading to short-run and long-run macroeconomic equilibrium gives a basic description of business cycles and the forces that tend to move the economy toward full employment in the long run, there are differences of opinion on how well this process works and the time lags between the short run and the long run.

The **classical economists** believed that shifts in both aggregate demand and aggregate supply were primarily driven by changes in technology over time. Although classical economists did not use the aggregate supply-aggregate demand analysis we have presented, their view of macroeconomic equilibrium is consistent with this analysis. We just need to add the assumption that the long-run adjustment of money wages to restore full-employment equilibrium happens fairly rapidly and that the economy therefore has a strong tendency toward full-employment equilibrium, as either recession or over-full employment lead to decreases or increases in the money wage rate. Their analysis concluded that taxes were the primary impediment to long-run equilibrium and that if the distortions in incentives from taxes were minimized, the economy would grow in an efficient manner with increases in labor and capital and with improvements in technology.

The Great Depression of the 1930s did not support the view of the classical economists. The economy in the United States operated significantly below its full-employment level for many years. Additionally, business cycles in general were more severe and more prolonged than the classical model would suggest. John Maynard Keynes was an economist who attempted to explain the depression and the nature of business cycles and to provide policy recommendations for moving the economy toward full-employment GDP and reducing the severity and duration of business cycles.

Keynes believed that shifts in aggregate demand due to changes in expectations were the primary cause of business cycles and that wages were "downward sticky," reducing the ability of a decrease in money wages to increase SAS and move the economy from recession (or depression) back towards the full-employment level of output. The *New Keynesians* added to this model, asserting that the prices of other productive inputs

©2010 Kaplan, Inc.

in addition to labor are also "downward sticky," presenting another barrier to the restoration of full-employment equilibrium.

The policy prescription of **Keynesian economists** was to directly increase aggregate demand through monetary policy (increasing the money supply) or through fiscal policy (increasing government spending, decreasing taxes, or both).

A third view of macroeconomic equilibrium is that held by **monetarists**. Monetarists believe that the main factor leading to business cycles and deviations from full-employment equilibrium is monetary policy. They suggest that to keep aggregate demand stable and growing, the central bank should follow a policy of steady and predictable increases in the money supply. Monetarists believe that recessions are caused by inappropriate decreases in the money supply and that recessions can be persistent because money wage rates are downward sticky (as do the Keynesians). Like the classical economists, however, they believe that the best tax policy is to keep taxes low to minimize the disruption and distortion that they introduce into the economy and the resulting decrease in full-employment GDP.

Study Session 5

KEY CONCEPTS

LOS 23.a

Long-run aggregate supply is vertical at potential (full-employment) real GDP and can change as a result of changes in the labor force, the amount of capital in the economy, or in technology.

Short-run aggregate supply is an increasing function of the price level, is affected by the same factors that affect long-run aggregate supply, and is constructed holding the money wage rate constant. Money wages are assumed to depend directly on workers' expectations about the future rate of inflation.

LOS 23.b

Aggregate demand is a decreasing function of the price level. Aggregate demand will increase with increases in incomes, a decrease in a country's exchange rate, or a rise in the expected rate of inflation. Expansionary monetary or fiscal policy can both increase aggregate demand.

LOS 23.c

From an initial long-run equilibrium, an increase (decrease) in aggregate demand will increase (decrease) the price level and output in the short run, and the resulting increase (decrease) in money wages as workers' inflation expectations adjust to the new rate of inflation will decrease (increase) short-run aggregate supply, resulting in further price level increases (decreases) and a return to full-employment long-run equilibrium.

LOS 23.d

The classical economists believed that the adjustment of money wages to restore full-employment equilibrium is rapid and that without the distorting effects of taxes, long-run equilibrium real output would increase with increases in the labor force and accumulated capital, and with improvements in technology.

Keynesian economists believe that changes in expectations shift aggregate demand, which causes business cycles, and that because wages are "downward sticky," the economy may not return rapidly from recession to full-employment real GDP. Their policy prescription is to increase aggregate demand directly by expanding the money supply or increasing the government deficit.

Monetarists believe that economic cycles are caused by inappropriate monetary policy and that a policy of steady and predictable increases in the money supply, together with low taxes, will lead to stability and maximum growth of real GDP.

CONCEPT CHECKERS

1. The economy's potential rate of output is *best* represented by:
    A. long-run aggregate supply.
    B. short-run aggregate supply.
    C. long-run aggregate demand.

2. Which of these factors is *least likely* to cause a shift in long-run aggregate supply?
    A. Warfare destroys a large number of factories.
    B. Prices of raw materials for production decrease.
    C. An advance in technology increases the rate of productivity.

3. Aggregate demand is *least likely* to include total:
    A. net imports.
    B. investment spending.
    C. government purchases.

4. Which of the following factors would be *least likely* to shift the aggregate demand curve?
    A. The federal deficit expands.
    B. Expected inflation decreases.
    C. The price level increases.

5. In short-run equilibrium, if aggregate demand is increasing faster than long-run aggregate supply:
    A. the price level is likely to increase.
    B. downward pressure on wages should ensue.
    C. supply will increase to meet the additional demand.

6. Which school of economic thought holds that unpredictable changes in central bank policy are the primary cause of business cycles?
    A. Classical.
    B. Keynesian.
    C. Monetarist.

ANSWERS – CONCEPT CHECKERS

1. **A**   The LRAS curve is vertical at the level of potential GDP.

2. **B**   Price changes for productive resources shift the short-run aggregate supply curve, but they do not affect long-run aggregate supply. LAS is influenced by changes in the quantity of labor, the quantity of capital, and the level of technology.

3. **A**   The foreign trade component of aggregate demand is net exports, or exports minus imports.

4. **C**   Since the Y axis of the aggregate supply/demand model is the price level, a change in the price level is a movement along the AD curve. As long as inflationary expectations are unchanged, an increase in the price level will not shift the aggregate demand curve.

5. **A**   If AD is increasing faster than LAS, the economy is expanding faster than its full-employment rate of output. This will cause pressure on wages and resource prices and lead to an increase in the price level. The SAS curve will shift to the left—a decrease in supply for any given price level—until the rate of output growth slows to its full-employment potential.

6. **C**   Monetarists believe that monetary policy is the main factor leading to business cycles and deviations from full-employment equilibrium.

The following is a review of the Economics principles designed to address the learning outcome statements set forth by CFA Institute®. This topic is also covered in:

MONEY, THE PRICE LEVEL, AND INFLATION

EXAM FOCUS

Here we address equilibrium short-term interest rates in the money market. On the supply side, the definition of the money supply and how an increase in reserves increases the money supply with a fractional reserve banking system are important concepts. On the demand side, you need to know how changes in real GDP and financial innovation affect the demand for money. Finally, we cover the determination of the short-term interest rate, how the quantity of money affects the growth of real GDP, and how the quantity theory of money can be interpreted in terms of the aggregate supply–aggregate demand model. Understanding these concepts and relations is very important to understanding subsequent topic reviews on the monetary policy of the U.S. Federal Reserve and on the goals and methods of central banks in general.

LOS 24.a: Explain the functions of money.

Money has three basic functions:

1. Money functions as a **medium of exchange** or **means of payment** because it is accepted as payment for goods and services. Compare this to a barter economy, where if someone has a goat and wants an ox, he has to find someone willing to trade one for the other (and imagine no eBay). With money, it is possible to sell the goat and buy the ox with the money received.

2. Money functions as a **unit of account** because prices of all goods and services are expressed in units of money; dollars, yen, rupees, pesos, and so forth. This allows us to determine how much of any good we are foregoing when consuming another.

3. Money functions as a **store of value** because I can work for money now, save it, and use the value of my labor later. Money preserves value better when inflation is low.

LOS 24.b: Describe the components of the M1 and M2 measures of money and discuss why checks and credit cards are not counted as money.

Two primary measures of the money supply in the United States are **M1 and M2**.

1. M1 includes all currency not held at banks, travelers' checks, and checking account deposits of individuals and firms (but not government checking accounts).

2. M2 includes all the components of M1, plus time deposits, savings deposits, and money market mutual fund balances.

Checking account deposits are counted as money, but outstanding checks are not. A check is simply an order to transfer money from one owner to another. Writing a check does not increase the money supply.

Likewise, using a credit card does not increase the money supply. A credit card transaction is, in effect, a short-term loan where the cardholder agrees to transfer money to the card issuer when the bill comes due. Even though a credit card is a means of carrying out transactions, it is not money.

LOS 24.c: Describe the economic functions of and differentiate among the various depository institutions and explain the impact of financial regulation, deregulation, and innovation.

There are three primary types of depository institutions:

1. **Commercial banks** essentially operate as intermediaries between savers and borrowers. Savers make deposits in banks to keep their money safe but also to earn a return on their savings. Banks take the deposits and put a proportion of those deposits to work by buying short-term securities such as Treasury bills, by investing in longer-term securities such as Treasury and corporate bonds, and by making loans. In a fractional reserve banking system, the bank must hold a specified proportion of deposits in reserve, as cash or (in the United States) deposits with the Federal Reserve Bank. This allows the bank to meet customer needs for withdrawals and still earn a return on the deposits not committed to reserves. The bank must manage the risk of its portfolio of loans and other assets to make sufficient interest income to be competitive but, at the same time, not take on risk that its depositors would consider excessive.

2. The terms **thrifts** and **thrift institutions** refer to savings banks, credit unions, and savings and loan associations (S&Ls). An S&L offers both checking and savings accounts and makes loans of various types using customer deposits.

3. A **money market mutual fund** is technically an investment company. *Money market* is usually used to refer to debt securities with maturities of one year or less. A money market mutual fund manages the pooled funds of many investors, investing it in short-term debt securities to preserve the fund's value and earn returns for the investors. Investors (depositors) have ready access to their funds, but some funds restrict liquidity by imposing minimum check amounts or a maximum number of withdrawals each month. Offering less liquidity keeps expenses down and consequently increases returns (interest earned).

Depository institutions have four main economic functions:

1. They *create liquidity* by using the funds from (short-term) deposits to make loans or purchase debt securities.

2. By acting as *financial intermediaries,* depository institutions lower the cost of funds for borrowers, compared to the cost if borrowers had to seek out lenders on their own.

3. Depository institutions are in a better position than individuals would be to *monitor the risk* of loans.

4. Institutions *pool the default risks* of individual loans by holding a portfolio of loans.

In the United States, bank and S&L deposits are insured in the event of failure of the institution to a maximum of $100,000 by the Federal Deposit Insurance Corporation (FDIC). The FDIC imposes restrictions on the institutions to manage the risk of insuring them against failure. Since the existence of deposit insurance significantly reduces the incentive for depositors to monitor the risk of an institution's portfolio, there is significant regulation of banks with respect to their balance sheets in four primary areas:

1. A minimum amount of equity (owners') capital must be maintained to give owners strong incentives to manage the risk of their asset portfolio well.

2. **Reserve requirements** set a minimum percentage of deposits (different for different types of accounts) that must be retained by the institution, either in cash or as deposits with the (U.S.) Federal Reserve.

3. There are restrictions on the types of deposits (e.g., savings deposits versus checking deposits) that the various institutions may accept.

4. There are rules about the proportions of various types of loans that the institutions can make. An example would be a restriction on the proportion of, or prohibition of, commercial loans. These restrictions differ by type of institution as well.

During the 1980s and 1990s, many of the restrictions that made commercial banks different from savings banks and thrifts were relaxed, which allowed the latter to compete more directly with the former and allowed other institutions to participate in activities which were formerly only permitted to banks and savings institutions. This decrease in regulation was accompanied by a high degree of financial innovation. Financial innovation refers to the introduction of new financial products, both for depositors and for those seeking debt capital. By introducing variable-rate mortgages, S&Ls were able to transfer some of the risk of rising inflation and rising interest rates to the borrowers of the funds. Computers have significantly reduced the cost of credit and debit card transactions and led to huge growth in these markets. The capacity of large banks to process millions of electronic transactions and checks at low cost with innovative computer systems was also a factor in the wave of mergers and acquisitions. Cost savings were realized when all institutions did not have to provide this capacity individually. The widespread use of ATMs and internet banking are further examples of the financial innovation that has grown out of technological advances.

Some innovation has been specifically adopted to avoid or circumvent regulation. New account types have been introduced to circumvent Regulation Q, which prohibits banks from paying interest on checking account deposits.

Overall, financial innovation has led to a shift from checking account deposits at commercial banks to checking account deposits at thrifts. Money market fund deposits have expanded tremendously, with a consequent decline in savings account deposits.

LOS 24.d: Explain the goals of the U.S. Federal Reserve (Fed) in conducting monetary policy and how the Fed uses its policy tools to control the quantity of money, and describe the assets and liabilities on the Fed's balance sheet.

The goals of the U.S. Federal Reserve are to manage the money supply in such a way as to keep inflation low and at the same time, promote economic growth and full employment. Additionally, the Fed attempts to reduce the magnitude of the expansions and recessions that make up business cycles.

One of the ways the Fed attempts to reach these goals is to target the **federal funds rate**. This is the rate at which banks make short-term (typically overnight) loans of reserves to other banks. The Fed influences the federal funds rate, which is a market-determined rate, through changes in the money supply.

The three **policy tools of the Federal Reserve** are:

1. In the United States, banks can borrow funds from the Fed if they have temporary shortfalls in reserves. The **discount rate** is the rate at which banks can borrow reserves from the Fed. A lower rate makes reserves less costly to banks, encourages lending, and tends to decrease interest rates. A higher discount rate has the opposite effect, raising interest rates.

2. **Bank reserve requirements** are the percentage of deposits that banks must retain (not loan out). By increasing the percentage of deposits banks are required to retain as reserves, the Fed effectively decreases the funds that are available for lending. This decrease in the amount available for lending will tend to increase interest rates. A decrease in the percentage reserve requirement will increase the funds available for loans, which tends to decrease interest rates. This tool only works well if banks are willing to lend, and customers are willing to borrow, the additional funds made available by reducing the reserve requirement.

3. **Open market operations** are the buying or selling of Treasury securities by the Fed in the open market. When the Fed buys securities, cash replaces securities in investor accounts, banks have excess reserves, more funds are available for lending, and interest rates decrease. Sales of securities by the Fed have the opposite effect, reducing cash balances and funds available for lending, and increasing interest rates. This is the Fed's most commonly used tool and is important in achieving the federal funds target rate.

The Fed's Balance Sheet

The assets of the U.S. Federal Reserve consist of:

*   Gold, deposits with other central banks, and special drawing rights at the International Monetary Fund.
*   U.S. Treasury bills, notes, and bonds.
*   Loans to banks (reserves loaned at the discount rate).

The most important of these is U.S. government securities, which are almost 90% of the Fed's assets.

The great majority (over 90%) of the liabilities of the Federal Reserve are Federal Reserve notes, that is, U.S. currency in circulation. Bank reserve deposits are a small part of the Fed's liabilities.

LOS 24.e: Discuss the creation of money, including the role played by excess reserves, and calculate the amount of loans a bank can generate, given new deposits.

In a **fractional reserve banking** system, such as the Fed system, a bank is only required to hold a fraction of its deposits in reserve. The **required reserve ratio** is used to measure the reserve requirement. Deposits in excess of the required reserve (**excess reserves**) may be loaned.

When a bank makes a loan, the borrower spends the money. The sellers who received the cash may deposit it in their banks. This action creates additional loanable funds, because only a fractional amount of the deposit is required by law to be held in reserve. This process of lending, spending, and depositing can continue until the amount of excess reserves available for lending is zero. This is referred to as the *multiplier effect*.

For example, assume that the required reserve ratio is 25%, and a bank finds itself with $1,000 in excess reserves. The bank can only lend out its own excess reserves of $1,000. If the borrower of the $1,000 deposits the cash in a second bank, the second bank will be able to lend its excess reserves of (0.75 × $1,000) = $750. Those funds may be deposited in a third bank, which can then lend its excess reserve of (0.75 × $750) = $563. If this lending and depositing continues, the money supply can expand to [(1 / 0.25) × $1,000] = $4,000. One dollar of excess reserves can generate a $4 increase in the money supply.

LOS 24.f: Describe the monetary base and explain the relation among the monetary base, the money multiplier, and the quantity of money.

The **monetary base** includes Federal Reserve notes, coins (issued by the U.S. Treasury), and banks' reserve deposits at the Fed.

When the Fed uses open market operations to expand the monetary base, the quantity of money increases with a multiplier effect because the increase (decrease) in bank deposits when the fed buys (sells) securities creates excess reserves. The magnitude of the expansion of the money supply is reduced by the portion of securities proceeds and bank loans that are held in cash. The effect of people holding part of the increase in the money supply as currency, rather than depositing it so that it can be used to create more loans, is called a **currency drain**.

The **money multiplier** for a change in the monetary base thus depends on both the required reserve ratio and the currency drain:

$$\text{money multiplier} = \frac{(1 + c)}{(r + c)}$$

where c is currency as a percentage of deposits and r is the required reserve ratio. The relation among the monetary base, the money multiplier, and the quantity of money can be stated as:

change in quantity of money = change in monetary base × money multiplier

LOS 24.g: Explain the factors that influence the demand for money and describe the demand for money curve, including the effects of changes in real GDP and financial innovation.

There are different definitions of money. For our purposes here, we define it as currency in circulation, checking account deposits, and traveler's checks—balances held in the form of ready cash.

When households and firms earn income, they convert some of it into goods for consumption or production, and set aside the rest. They can either hold this remaining amount as cash balances or use it to earn interest income by depositing it in a bank savings account or buying interest bearing securities.

How much households and firms choose to hold in cash balances, or their **demand for money**, is largely determined by interest rates. Think of the interest that could be earned on money deposited in a savings account or money market fund as the opportunity cost of holding money (cash balances).

The relation between short-term interest rates and the quantity of money that firms and households demand to hold is illustrated in Figure 1, where the downward slope indicates that at lower interest rates, firms and households choose to hold more money. At higher interest rates, the opportunity cost of holding money increases, and firms and households will desire to hold less money and more interest bearing financial assets.

The **supply of money** is determined by the central bank (the Fed in the United States) and is independent of the interest rate. This accounts for the vertical (perfectly inelastic) supply curve in Figure 1.

Figure 1: The Supply and Demand for Money

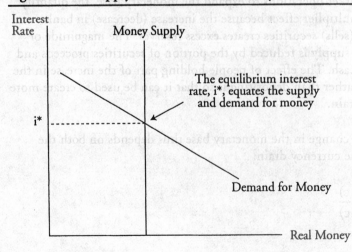

©2010 Kaplan, Inc.

Now if we measure the money supply in nominal currency units, it will be sensitive to the price level. As inflation increases, households and businesses need more money to buy costlier goods and services. If prices doubled, firms and households would need approximately twice the amount of money to fund their purchases and to meet their needs for money in reserve. If we divide the nominal supply of money by the price level (a price index), we have the money supply in real terms. We can think of the real money supply as the money supply in terms of constant purchasing power. The equilibrium interest rate in Figure 1, i^*, is the interest rate for which the demand to hold real money balances is just equal to the real money supply.

If real gross domestic product (GDP) rises, more goods and services are bought and sold, and more money is needed to conduct these transactions. Increases in real GDP shift the money demand curve up. Decreases in real GDP shift it down so that less money is demanded at each level of interest rates.

The increased use of credit cards and debit cards, the availability of interest-bearing checking accounts, easier transfer of funds from savings to checking, the proliferation of ATMs, and internet banking and bill paying are all financial innovations that have affected the demand for money curve. Overall, financial innovation has reduced the demand for money below what it would have been if only the increase in real GDP was at work. The increased use of credit cards and the proliferation of ATMs have likely been the most important innovations with respect to the demand for money.

LOS 24.h: Explain interest rate determination and the short-run and long-run effects of money on real GDP.

Interest rates are determined by the equilibrium between money supply and money demand. As illustrated in Figure 2, if the interest rate is above the equilibrium rate (i_{high}), there is excess supply of real money. Firms and households are holding more real money balances than they desire to, given the opportunity cost of holding money balances. They will purchase securities to reduce their money balances, which will decrease the interest rate as securities prices are bid up. If interest rates are below equilibrium (i_{low}), there is excess demand for real money balances, as illustrated in Figure 2. Firms and households will sell securities to increase their money holdings to the desired level, decreasing securities prices and increasing the interest rate.

Figure 2: Disequilibrium in the Money Market

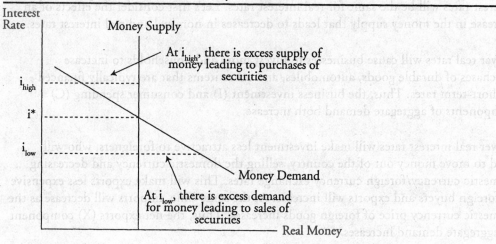

Let's look at how the central bank can affect interest rates by examining the effects of open market operations on the equilibrium interest rate when the money supply is changed. Consider a situation where the central bank wants to decrease short-term interest rates and will do so by buying securities in the open market. The cash paid for the securities increases the real money supply and bank reserves, which leads to a further increase in the real money supply as banks make loans based on the increase in excess reserves. This shifts the real money supply curve to the right as illustrated in Figure 3. At the previous equilibrium interest rate of 5%, there is now excess supply of money balances. To reduce their money holdings, firms and households buy securities, increasing securities prices and decreasing interest rates until the new equilibrium interest rate in Figure 3 (4%) is achieved. Of course, if the central bank sold securities to decrease the money supply, excess demand for real money balances would result in sales of securities and an increase in the interest rate.

Figure 3: An Increase in the Money Supply Decreases the Interest Rate

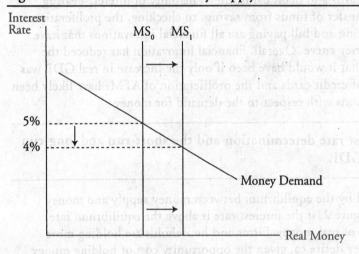

Short-Run and Long-Run Effects of Money on Real GDP

Now that we have determined the effects of monetary policy changes (changes in the money supply) on nominal interest rates, we turn our attention to the effect on the overall economy. In the short run, the effects of money supply changes on nominal interest rates will be the same for real interest rates. Let's first consider the effects of an increase in the money supply that leads to decreases in nominal and real interest rates.

Lower real rates will cause businesses to invest more and households to increase purchases of durable goods, automobiles, and other items that are typically financed at short-term rates. Thus, the business investment (I) and consumer spending (C) components of aggregate demand both increase.

Lower real interest rates will make investment less attractive to foreigners, who will tend to move money out of the country, selling the domestic currency and decreasing domestic currency/foreign currency exchange rates. This will make exports less expensive to foreign buyers and exports will increase. At the same time, imports will decrease as the domestic currency price of foreign goods increases. Thus, the net exports (X) component of aggregate demand increases.

The effect of the interest rate decrease in the short run will be even stronger because there is a multiplier effect. The increase in aggregate demand and expenditures will cause incomes to go up, which further increases consumption and investment. This spending on investment and consumption, in turn, also increases (someone's) income. This process is repeated and, even though not all of each consumer's increase in income is used to increase consumption, the eventual effect on consumption and aggregate demand will be much greater than the initial increase in consumption and aggregate demand.

This increase in aggregate demand will increase real GDP and the price level, as we saw in our analysis of the aggregate supply-aggregate demand model. Action by the central bank to decrease the money supply and increase rates will have the opposite effect. Rising rates will reduce household purchases, business investment, net exports, and aggregate demand, resulting in a decrease in real GDP and the price level.

If the economy is operating at the full-employment level (long-run aggregate supply) when the central bank increases the money supply, the increase in real GDP must be temporary. Recall that when an increase in aggregate demand increases real GDP above full-employment GDP, money wages and the cost of other productive resources will rise, causing a shift to a new short-run aggregate supply curve. Thus, the long-run effect of an increase in the money supply will simply be an increase in the price level (rate of inflation) as the economy returns to full-employment GDP on the long-run aggregate supply curve. This is illustrated in Figure 4. Panel (b) is the same initial and long-run response to an increase in aggregate demand (from AD_0 to AD_1) that we saw in the review of aggregate supply and aggregate demand. Initially, the price level rises to P_1, and the resulting increase in inflation decreases the real wage so that SAS shifts from SAS_0 to SAS_1. The new long-run equilibrium real GDP is back to potential real GDP (along LAS) and the price level has increased to P_2. Note that when the price level has increased to P_2, the increase in the price level has just offset the increase in the nominal money supply, so the real money supply returns to MS_0. This long-run adjustment is illustrated in panel (a). As a result of this decrease in the real money supply, the equilibrium interest rate returns to its original equilibrium level of 5% in Figure 4.

Figure 4: An Increase in the Money Supply at Full-Employment GDP

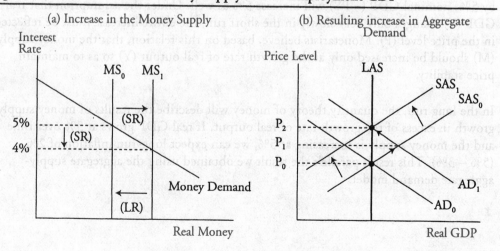

LOS 24.i: Discuss the quantity theory of money and its relation to aggregate supply and aggregate demand.

If we break GDP into the price level and its real output component (price × real output), we obtain an identity known as the **equation of exchange**, which is:

money supply × velocity = GDP = price × real output

Velocity is the average number of times per year each dollar is used to buy goods and services (velocity = GDP / money). Therefore, the money supply multiplied by velocity must equal nominal GDP. The equation of exchange must hold with velocity defined in this way. The equation of exchange may be symbolically expressed as:

$$MV = PY$$

where:
M = money supply
V = velocity
P = price
Y = real output

The **quantity theory of money** states that an increase in the money supply will cause a proportional increase in prices. The original proponents of the quantity theory felt that velocity and output were determined by institutional factors other than the money supply and were thus nearly constant. Therefore, if the money supply increases while velocity and quantities are fixed, prices must rise. Rearranging the equation of exchange, we get:

$$P = M\left(\frac{V}{Y}\right)$$

Since velocity (V) and real output (Y) change very slowly, an increase in the money supply (M) must result in a proportional increase in prices (inflation). If we increase M by 5%, nominal GDP (= PY) will increase 5% as well. Under the assumption that real GDP (Y) changes only very slowly in the short run, the entire increase must be reflected in the price level (P). Monetarists believe, based on this relation, that the money supply (M) should be increased only at the growth rate of real output (Y) so as to maintain price stability.

In the long run, the quantity theory of money will describe the results of money supply growth in excess of the growth rate of real output. If real GDP grows at 3% over time and the money supply is increasing at 5%, we can expect long-run inflation of 2% (5% – 3%). This result parallels the result we obtained using the aggregate supply-aggregate demand model.

©2010 Kaplan, Inc.

KEY CONCEPTS

LOS 24.a

Money has three basic functions:

- Medium of exchange: Money is accepted as payment for goods and services.
- Unit of account: Prices are expressed in units of money, allowing us to determine how much consumption of one good we are foregoing when consuming another.
- Store of value: Money can be saved and consumption delayed to a later period.

LOS 24.b

M1 and M2 are measures of the U.S. money supply. M1 includes currency, travelers' checks, and checking deposits of individuals and firms. M2 includes M1, time deposits, savings deposits, and money market mutual funds.

Checks and credit cards are not part of the money supply. Checks are orders to transfer money (M1) from one owner to another. Credit cards are a means of obtaining an immediate short-term loan and represent a promise to pay, not payment.

LOS 24.c

Commercial banks, thrift institutions, and money market funds all act as intermediaries in lending the funds of savers to borrowers of various types.

Financial innovation involves the introduction of new products to better serve customer needs and increase the profit of intermediaries by decreasing borrowing costs and increasing earnings from lending. These innovations are driven by changes in the economic environment, technology, and regulation.

LOS 24.d

The U.S. Federal Reserve has a mandate to manage the money supply in such a way as to produce low inflation, full employment, and economic growth.

The Fed can increase (decrease) the money supply by buying (selling) Treasury securities in the open market, decreasing (increasing) the discount rate, or decreasing (increasing) the required reserve ratio.

Assets on the Fed's balance sheet consist primarily of U.S. Treasury securities, but also include gold, IMF special drawing rights, and loans to banks. The Fed's liabilities are primarily U.S. currency (Federal Reserve notes) but also include banks' reserve deposits.

LOS 24.e

In a fractional reserve banking system, banks must hold a percentage of their deposits as required reserves and may lend out the rest (excess reserves). When new reserves are added to the system, a system of fractional reserves allows the banking system to increase the money supply by a multiple of new reserves, equal to the reciprocal of the required reserve ratio.

LOS 24.f

The monetary base consists of currency (Federal Reserve notes, coins) and banks' deposits at the Fed.

Changes in the monetary base change the quantity of money with a multiplier effect, which is a function of both the required reserve ratio and the currency drain (loan proceeds withdrawn from the banking system).

LOS 24.g

The demand to hold money is a decreasing function of the interest rate that can be earned on short-term securities.

The demand for money increases with real GDP and with the price level.

Innovations such as credit and debit cards and automated teller machines have tended to reduce the demand for money.

LOS 24.h

The money supply is controlled by the central bank and equilibrium interest rates are determined by the intersection of the supply and demand for money.

An increase (decrease) in the money supply will result in an excess supply of (demand for) money, leading individuals and businesses to buy (sell) securities, driving securities prices up (down) and decreasing (increasing) equilibrium interest rates.

In the short run, decreases (increases) in the equilibrium interest rate from increases (decreases) in the money supply will increase (decrease) aggregate demand, which will increase (decrease) real GDP and the price level. In the long run, money supply growth has no effect on real GDP.

LOS 24.i

The quantity theory of money is based on the equation of exchange (MV = PY) and an assumption that GDP growth and money velocity are relatively constant, so that increases in the money supply when the economy is operating at potential (full-employment) GDP will lead to a proportional increase in prices.

CONCEPT CHECKERS

1. Which of the following statements is *least accurate*? The existence and use of money:
   A. permits individuals to perform economic calculations.
   B. requires the central bank to control the supply of currency.
   C. increases the efficiency of transactions as against a barter system.

2. The M1 measure of the money supply is *least likely* to include:
   A. savings account deposits.
   B. checking account deposits.
   C. currency held by the public.

3. Depository institutions *least likely* include:
   A. growth funds.
   B. credit unions.
   C. commercial banks.

4. Banks and savings institutions lower the cost of funds for borrowers by saving them the time and expense of finding numerous individuals who are willing to lend to them. This statement *best* describes the depository institutions' function as:
   A. exchange media.
   B. liquidity creators.
   C. financial intermediaries.

5. Assume the Federal Reserve purchases $1 billion in securities in the open market. What is the maximum increase in the money supply that can result from this action, if the required reserve ratio is 15% and there is no currency drain?
   A. $850 million.
   B. $1 billion.
   C. $6.67 billion.

6. The policy tool the Federal Reserve uses *most* often is:
   A. the discount rate.
   B. reserve requirements.
   C. open market operations.

7. The goals and targets of Federal Reserve policy *least likely* include:
   A. promoting economic growth and full employment.
   B. maintaining stable exchange rates.
   C. managing the money supply in such a way as to keep inflation low.

8. The money demand schedule slopes downward to the right, showing that:
   A. an expansion in the money supply increases interest rates.
   B. as the opportunity cost of holding money rises, people want to hold less money.
   C. a reduction in the money supply reduces the interest rate.

9. The money supply schedule is vertical because the:
    A. money supply is dependent upon interest rates.
    B. demand schedule is downward-sloping.
    C. money supply is independent of interest rates.

10. Which of the following statements is *most likely* accurate? Money:
    A. demand rises with nominal interest rates.
    B. demand rises with nominal income.
    C. supply rises with nominal interest rates.

11. If money supply and demand are in equilibrium and the central bank sells securities in the open market:
    A. bank reserves will increase.
    B. short-term interest rates will decrease.
    C. firms and households will sell securities for cash.

12. The *most likely* long-term effect of an increase in the money supply when the economy is at full-employment GDP is:
    A. higher output.
    B. higher prices.
    C. lower unemployment.

13. If the money supply is rising and velocity is falling:
    A. prices will fall.
    B. real GDP will rise.
    C. the impact on prices and real GDP is uncertain.

14. According to the quantity theory of money:
    A. real output and velocity are independent of the money supply.
    B. real output and velocity increase with the money supply.
    C. an increase in the money stock will decrease gross domestic product.

15. According to the quantity theory of money, if nominal GDP is $7.0 trillion and the money supply is $1.0 trillion, then the velocity of the money supply is *closest* to:
    A. 0.1.
    B. 7.0.
    C. 8.0.

ANSWERS – CONCEPT CHECKERS

1. **B** Money functions as a unit of account, a medium of exchange, and a store of value. Money existed long before the idea of central banking was conceived.

2. **A** Savings deposits are a component of M2. M1 includes currency not held at banks, travelers' checks, and checking account deposits of individuals and businesses.

3. **A** The only kind of investment company that would be considered a depository institution is a money market mutual fund.

4. **C** By acting as financial intermediaries, depository institutions lower the cost of funds for borrowers from what they would be if they had to seek out individuals willing to lend.

5. **C** The potential money supply expansion multiple is 1 / 0.15 = 6.67, so the open market purchase can increase the money supply by a maximum of $6.67 billion.

6. **C** Open market operations are the Fed's most commonly used tool.

7. **B** The Fed does not target exchange rates and has no mandate to maintain stable exchange rates.

8. **B** With interest rates on the vertical axis and the quantity of real money on the horizontal axis, the downward slope of the money demand schedule shows that as the opportunity cost of holding money rises, people want to hold less money. People would prefer to invest money in bonds and CDs rather than hold cash when interest rates are high.

9. **C** The money supply schedule is vertical because the money supply is independent of interest rates. The Fed controls the money supply.

10. **B** Money demand rises with nominal income. As income increases, either because of inflation or increases in real output, more money is needed in the economy to conduct transactions.

11. **C** If the central bank sells securities, it is decreasing the money supply. This will reduce bank reserves. Firms and households will have lower cash balances than they wish to hold at equilibrium, so they sell securities, decreasing securities prices and increasing interest rates to their new equilibrium level.

12. **B** The long-term effect of an increase in the money supply when the economy is at full-employment GDP will be higher prices. Although output and employment will increase in the short run, they will return to potential real GDP levels in the long run.

13. **C** An increase in the money supply is consistent with an increase in nominal GDP. However, a decrease in velocity is consistent with a decrease in nominal GDP. Unless we know the size of the changes in the two variables, there is no way to tell what the net impact is on real GDP and prices.

14. **A** According to the quantity theory of money, real output and velocity are independent of the money supply. As a result, an increase in the money supply increases prices.

15. **B**   The equation of exchange is: $MV = PY$

Here, $GDP = PY$, so that $MV = GDP$

Therefore, (1.0 trillion)$(V) = \$7.0$ trillion

$V = \$7.0$ trillion $/\$1.0$ trillion

$V = 7.0$

The following is a review of the Economics principles designed to address the learning outcome statements set forth by CFA Institute®. This topic is also covered in:

U.S. Inflation, Unemployment, and Business Cycles

Exam Focus

This is all key material. Defining inflation, measuring inflation, and knowing the difference in the effects of anticipated and unanticipated inflation are all important. Take the time to understand the difference between demand-pull and cost-push inflation in the context of the aggregate supply-aggregate demand model. This review ties together earlier material on nominal interest rates, expected inflation, and the rate of growth of the money supply.

LOS 25.a: Differentiate between inflation and the price level.

Inflation is a persistent increase in the price level over time. Inflation erodes the purchasing power of a currency. If it accelerates unchecked, inflation ultimately can destroy a country's monetary system, forcing individuals and businesses to adopt foreign money or revert to bartering physical goods.

The key word in our definition is "persistent." If the price level increases in a single jump but does not continue rising, the economy is not experiencing inflation. An increase in the price of a single good or in *relative* prices of some goods are not inflation. If inflation is present, the prices of almost all goods and services are increasing.

LOS 25.b: Describe and distinguish among the factors resulting in demand-pull and cost-push inflation and describe the evolution of demand-pull and cost-push inflationary processes.

The two types of inflation are **demand-pull** and **cost-push**. Demand-pull inflation results from an increase in aggregate demand, while cost-push inflation results from a decrease in aggregate supply.

Demand-Pull Inflation

Demand-pull inflation can result from an increase in the money supply, increased government spending, or any other cause that increases aggregate demand. Figure 1 shows the effect on the price level when aggregate demand increases (shifts to the right). In Figure 1, the economy begins at equilibrium with output at GDP_1 and the price level at P_1. The aggregate demand and short-run aggregate supply curves are AD_1 and $SRAS_1$. Real GDP is equal to potential GDP, which is represented by the long-run aggregate supply curve LRAS.

Figure 1: Demand-Pull Inflation

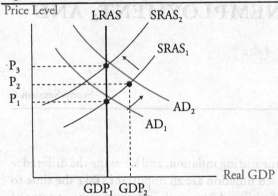

Now suppose the central bank increases the money supply, which increases aggregate demand to AD_2. With no initial change in aggregate supply, output increases to GDP_2 and the price level increases to P_2. Prices rise, and real GDP is above potential (full-employment) GDP.

With real GDP above its full-employment level, the increase in GDP is not sustainable. Unemployment falls below its natural rate, which puts upward pressure on real wages. Rising real wages result in a decrease in short-run aggregate supply (the curve shifts left from $SRAS_1$) until real GDP reverts back to full-employment GDP. The boom turns into a bust as output falls back to GDP_1, and the price level increases further to P_3.

In the absence of other changes, the economy would reach a new equilibrium price level at P_3. But what would happen if the central bank tried to keep GDP above the full-employment level with further increases in the money supply? The same results would occur repeatedly. Output could not remain above its potential in the long run, but the induced increase in aggregate demand and the resulting pressure on wages would keep the price level rising ever higher. Demand-pull inflation would persist until the central bank reduced the growth rate of the money supply and allowed the economy to return to full employment equilibrium at a level of real GDP equal to potential GDP.

Cost-Push Inflation

Inflation can also result from an initial decrease in aggregate supply caused by an increase in the real price of an important factor of production, such as wages or energy.

Figure 2 illustrates the effect on output and the price level of a decrease in aggregate supply. The reduction from $SRAS_1$ to $SRAS_2$ increases the price level to P_2, and with no initial change in aggregate demand, reduces output to GDP_2. The impact on output is the key difference between the demand-pull and cost-push effects: the demand-pull effect increases GDP above full-employment GDP, while cost-push inflation from a decrease in aggregate supply initially decreases GDP.

If the decline in GDP brings a policy response that stimulates aggregate demand so output returns to its long-run potential, the result would be a further increase in the price level to P_3.

The increase in the price level would only represent inflation if it persisted. For that to happen, the supply shock that caused SRAS to decrease would have to be repeated, and policy makers would have to keep responding by expanding the money supply. The oil crisis of the 1970s is an example of a cost-push inflation spiral.

Figure 2: Cost-Push Inflation

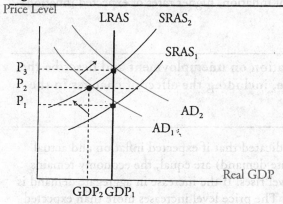

LOS 25.c: Explain the costs of anticipated inflation.

While the AS – AD model suggests that correctly anticipated rates of inflation are consistent with full-employment equilibrium real GDP without inflationary or recessionary gaps and cycles, high inflation can have negative effects on real output even when correctly anticipated. High inflation, even when anticipated, reduces economic output and the growth rate of GDP because it:

- Diverts resources from other productive activities to deal with inflation's effects and uncertainty.
- Decreases the value of currency in transactions and as a store of value.
- Reduces real after-tax returns from investment and savings (since nominal increases in value purely from inflation are taxed), which reduces savings and capital investment in the economy.

LOS 25.d: Explain the relation among inflation, nominal interest rates, and the demand and supply of money.

Recall that we previously defined the **nominal risk-free interest rate** as the sum of the real risk-free rate and the expected inflation rate. We now examine why this is necessarily so.

The nominal rate of interest is the equilibrium rate determined in the market for savings and investment. If expected inflation is higher, business will expect greater returns on their investments because they will factor in higher prices for their output in the future. At the same time, savers will require a greater rate of return on their savings because they are considering the trade-off between current consumption and future consumption. Since they are concerned with real consumption, they will require a greater nominal rate of return when the expected rate of inflation is higher, so that the real consumption that they receive in the future in return for not consuming now (saving) is the same. When presented in terms of nominal interest rates, this combination of an increase in demand for financial capital and a decrease in the supply of financial capital (savings) increases the equilibrium nominal rate of interest.

We have also related the actual inflation rate and, eventually, the expected inflation rate to the rate of growth of the money supply. We can conclude that higher rates of growth of the money supply lead to higher rates of inflation, higher rates of expected inflation, and higher nominal interest rates.

LOS 25.e: Explain the impact of inflation on unemployment and describe the short-run and long-run Phillips curve, including the effect of changes in the natural rate of unemployment.

Our analysis using the AS – AD model indicated that if expected inflation and actual inflation (based on the increase in aggregate demand) are equal, the economy remains at full-employment GDP and the price level rises. If the increase in aggregate demand is greater than expected, two things happen. The price level increases more than expected (actual inflation is greater than expected inflation), and unemployment decreases to a level below its natural rate. This negative relationship between unexpected inflation and unemployment is depicted in the **short-run Phillips curve** shown in Figure 3. The decrease in unemployment in the short run changes unemployment from its natural rate along the **long-run Phillips curve** to a point like 1. Note that each short-run Phillips curve is constructed holding the expected rate of inflation constant and for a particular natural rate of unemployment.

Figure 3: Long-Run and Short-Run Phillips Curve

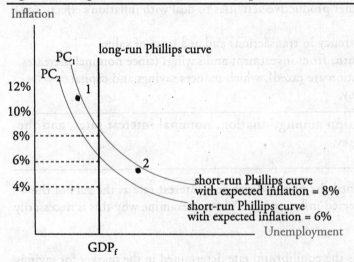

In the long run, expected inflation and actual inflation are equal so the economy is at full employment and the rate of unemployment is equal to its natural rate.

When a central bank unexpectedly decreases the rate of money supply growth to reduce inflation, the initial effect is to decrease aggregate supply as real wages rise, resulting in a short-run decrease in both GDP and employment. In this case, actual inflation is less than anticipated inflation, and unemployment increases as a result. This situation is represented by a movement along the short-run Phillips curve in Figure 3 to a point such as 2.

If the reduced rate of growth of the money supply is maintained, eventually the new lower rate of inflation is correctly anticipated in wage contracts, and the decrease in short-run aggregate supply and increase in aggregate demand are such that the economy remains at full-employment GDP. We represent this situation as a shift in the short-run Phillips curve to PC_2. Note that the short-run Phillips curve intersects the long-run Phillips curve at the expected rate of inflation. It is the short-run differences between expected inflation and actual inflation that are driving the relationship between unexpected inflation and unemployment in the short run.

Changes in the Natural Rate of Unemployment

Recall that the natural rate of unemployment consists of the frictional and structural unemployment that exists when cyclical unemployment is zero and output is at potential (full-employment) GDP. Changes in the natural rate can come from many sources, including the size and makeup of the labor force, changes that affect labor mobility, and advances in technology that replace some jobs and create new ones. An increase (decrease) in the natural rate would be represented as a shift to the right (left) in the long-run Phillips curve.

LOS 25.f: Explain how economic growth, inflation, and unemployment affect the business cycle.

The **business cycle** is characterized by fluctuations in economic activity. Real gross domestic product (GDP) and the rate of unemployment are the key variables used to determine the current phase of the cycle.

The business cycle has two phases: **expansion** (real GDP is increasing) and **contraction** or **recession** (real GDP is decreasing). The turning points between the phases are called the **peak** and the **trough** of the business cycle. The phases and turning points are illustrated in Figure 4.

Figure 4: Business Cycle

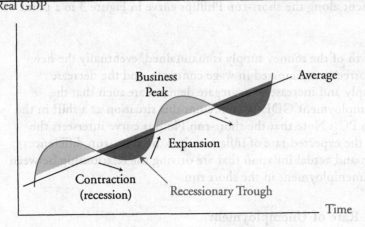

The National Bureau of Economic Research (NBER) is the agency that tracks the phases of the U.S. business cycle. NBER defines a recession as "a significant decline in economic activity spread across the economy, lasting more than a few months, normally visible in real GDP, real income, employment, industrial production, and wholesale-retail sales."[1] The NBER primarily uses measures of employment, industrial production, and personal income to determine whether the economy is expanding or contracting.

In an expansion, economic growth is positive, unemployment is decreasing, and inflationary pressures are increasing. The reverse is true in a contraction.

LOS 25.g: Describe mainstream business cycle theory and real business cycle (RBC) theory and distinguish between them, including the role of productivity changes.

There are two main schools of thought on the causes of business cycles. The mainstream view is that business cycles are caused by the variability of aggregate demand. Potential real GDP is believed to increase at a fairly stable rate over time. If aggregate demand increased at a steady rate as well, we would not observe business cycles of the magnitude that we do. However, aggregate demand sometimes grows more rapidly, and sometimes more slowly, than LRAS (potential GDP).

If aggregate demand grows more rapidly than LRAS, short-term equilibrium is along the short-run aggregate supply (SAS) curve at an output higher than potential full-employment GDP and a price level higher than the long-run equilibrium level. Unemployment is temporarily low, employment is temporarily over the full-employment level, and there is an inflationary gap. If aggregate demand grows more slowly than potential GDP, the new short-run equilibrium is at a level of output less than potential GDP, unemployment rises, and there is a recessionary gap.

These two situations are illustrated in Figure 5. An increase in potential GDP to LRAS$_1$ can be accompanied by an increase in aggregate demand to AD$_1$, in which

---

1. "The NBER's Recession Dating Procedure," October 21, 2003, available from the NBER Web site (www.nber.org/cycles/recessions.html).

©2010 Kaplan, Inc.

case employment and output increase to the new long-run equilibrium level, GDP_1. Alternatively, if the growth of aggregate demand is less (AD_L), output and employment are reduced and an economic contraction may result. If the growth of aggregate demand is high (greater than the increase in potential GDP), as with AD_H, the expansion in the economy is temporarily more rapid than the increase in potential GDP, and employment and output increase to the level labeled GDP_H.

Figure 5: Business Cycles, Mainstream View

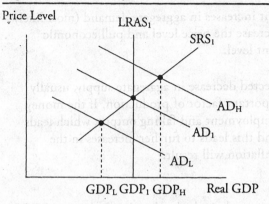

Why are there fluctuations in aggregate demand that lead to business cycles? Keynesian economists believe that these fluctuations are primarily due to swings in the level of optimism of those who run businesses. They overinvest and overproduce when they are too optimistic about future growth in potential GDP, and underinvest and underproduce when they are too pessimistic or fearful about the future growth of potential GDP.

Not surprisingly, monetarist economists believe that the variation in aggregate demand that causes business cycles is due to variation in the rate of growth of the money supply, likely from inappropriate decisions by the monetary authority. To this supposition, we must add that wages, and possibly prices of other productive inputs, are "sticky" so that rapid shifts of the SAS curve do not occur as wages change in response to inflationary or recessionary gaps.

New classical economists believe that only unexpected changes in aggregate demand lead to economic cycles. New Keynesian economists stress the importance of workers' rational expectations (based on past inflation) about inflation rates in determining the position of the SAS curve. In their view, both expected and unexpected changes in aggregate demand fuel economic cycles.

An alternative school of thought with respect to business cycles is termed **real business cycle theory** and emphasizes the effect of real economic variables as opposed to monetary variables or variation in expectations about aggregate demand growth. Under this theory, due to improvements in technology, workers' productivity sometimes grows rapidly and sometimes more slowly. This leads to fluctuations in the growth rate of potential real GDP, as opposed to the assumption of a steady increase in potential real GDP underlying the mainstream business cycle theories explained above. Rapid increases in productivity lead to economic expansions, and periods of slower increases in productivity lead to economic contractions.

KEY CONCEPTS

LOS 25.a

Inflation is a persistent increase in the price level over time, not a one-time increase in the price level or simply an increase in the prices of some goods or resources.

LOS 25.b

Demand-pull inflation results from persistent increases in aggregate demand (most likely from increases in the money supply) that increase the price level and pull economic output above its potential or full-employment level.

Cost-push inflation is initiated by an unexpected decrease in aggregate supply, usually the result of an increase in the cost of an important factor of production. If the money supply is increased in reaction to rising unemployment and falling output, which leads to a further increase in the resource price, and this leads to further increases in the money supply to restore full employment, inflation will result.

LOS 25.c

High inflation, even when well-anticipated, can reduce the level and growth rate of GDP by reducing real after-tax returns on investment, increasing transaction costs as currency is more costly to hold, and decreasing productive activity as individuals and businesses devote time and effort to dealing with uncertainty about the rate of inflation.

LOS 25.d

A premium for the expected inflation rate is reflected in all nominal interest rates and will depend in the long run on the rate of growth of the money supply. Higher rates of money supply growth lead to higher rates of inflation, higher rates of expected inflation, and higher nominal interest rates.

LOS 25.e

The short-run Phillips curve is constructed holding expected inflation and the natural rate of unemployment constant, and it illustrates the negative relationship between unexpected inflation and unemployment.

The long-run Phillips curve is vertical at the natural rate of unemployment, which can be affected by the size and makeup of the labor force, changes that affect labor mobility, and advances in technology that replace some jobs and create new ones.

LOS 25.f

Business cycles are characterized by periods of rapid economic growth, with increases in inflation and decreases in the unemployment rate, followed by periods of falling economic output, decreasing inflation, and rising unemployment.

LOS 25.g

Mainstream business cycle theory is based on the idea that potential real GDP (LRAS) increases steadily, but variation in aggregate demand results in cyclicality in the rates of output growth, price inflation, and unemployment.

Real business cycle theory is based on the idea that variation in the rate of growth of potential real GDP, due to changing rates of productivity growth (from technological change), results in cycles between higher and lower rates of growth of real GDP, employment, and inflation.

CONCEPT CHECKERS

1. A price index for the broad economy was at the following year-end levels over a 5-year period:

   Year 1   106.5
   Year 2   114.2
   Year 3   119.9
   Year 4   124.8
   Year 5   128.1

   Which statement *best* describes the behavior of inflation as measured by this index?
   A. Stable.
   B. Accelerating.
   C. Decelerating.

2. For a demand-pull effect or a cost-push effect to cause inflation:
   A. the AD curve has to shift in response to a shift of the AS curve.
   B. the cause of the shift in AD or AS must be repeated or sustained.
   C. economic equilibrium must be re-established at a higher price level.

3. An unexpected change in the rate of inflation causes:
   A. the long-run Phillips curve to shift.
   B. the short-run Phillips curve to shift.
   C. movement along the short-run Phillips curve.

Use the following data to answer Questions 4 and 5.

The unemployment rate in Fredonia is 7%, which economists estimate to be its natural rate. The inflation rate for the past year was 3%. Fredonia's policy makers believe they can reduce unemployment to a permanently lower rate by continually stimulating aggregate demand.

4. If Fredonia adopts this policy, what are the *most likely* short-run effects on inflation and unemployment?

Unemployment rate	Inflation rate
A. Less than 7%	More than 3%
B. Remains at 7%	Less than 3%
C. More than 7%	Remains at 3%

5. If Fredonia adopts this policy, what are the *most likely* long-run effects on inflation and unemployment?

Unemployment rate	Inflation rate
A. Less than 7%	Remains at 3%
B. More than 7%	Less than 3%
C. Remains at 7%	More than 3%

6. In year 1, the nominal interest rate was 10% and the expected rate of inflation was 7%. One year later, the nominal interest rate is 8% and inflation expectations are 6%. What has happened to real interest rates between year 1 and year 2? They:
    A. increased by 1%.
    B. decreased by 1%.
    C. decreased by 2%.

7. The contraction phase of the business cycle is *least likely* accompanied by:
    A. decreasing unemployment.
    B. decreasing inflation pressure.
    C. low or negative economic growth.

8. The theory that the rate of growth in potential GDP fluctuates because technology change leads to cycles in the rate of productivity growth is known as:
    A. real business cycle theory.
    B. new classical cycle theory.
    C. new Keynesian cycle theory.

ANSWERS – CONCEPT CHECKERS

1. **C** Using the formula for the inflation rate, we can calculate the inflation rate for years 2 to 5.

   Year 2   7.2%
   Year 3   5.0%
   Year 4   4.1%
   Year 5   2.6%

   Inflation was decelerating over this period.

2. **B** To cause more than a one-time increase in the price level, whatever caused the AD curve to shift to the right (demand-pull) or the AS curve to shift to the left (cost-push) must be sustained over time.

3. **C** An unexpected change in inflation causes the unemployment rate to move in the opposite direction. This represents movement along the short-run Phillips curve.

4. **A** If unemployment is at its natural rate, GDP growth is at its potential rate. Stimulating AD from this level increases output in the short run, which reduces unemployment but also increases the price level.

5. **C** In the long run, unemployment cannot be held below its natural rate. The stimulus to AD will result in wage pressures, forcing the AS curve to the left, reducing output back to its potential rate, increasing unemployment back to its natural rate, and increasing the price level further. As the vertical long-run Phillips curve shows, the higher inflation rate has no beneficial effect on the natural rate of unemployment.

6. **B** Because the nominal interest rate was 10% and the expected rate of inflation was 7% in the first year, the real rate of interest was 3% (10% – 7%). One year later, with the nominal interest rate at 8% and inflation expectations at 6%, the real rate of interest was 2% (8% – 6%). Therefore, the real interest rate decreased by 1% between year 1 and year 2.

7. **A** An economic contraction is likely to feature increasing unemployment (i.e., decreasing employment), along with declining economic output and decreasing inflationary pressure.

8. **A** Under real business cycle theory, the variation in the rate at which technological change increases labor productivity leads to periods of faster or slower growth in potential (full-employment) GDP. Mainstream business cycle theories, including the new Keynesian and new classical cycle theories, are based on an assumption that the rate of growth in potential GDP is stable over time.

FISCAL POLICY

Study Session 6

EXAM FOCUS

This topic review focuses on fiscal policy, which refers to the taxing and spending decisions of the government. Understand well how changes in taxing and government spending affect economic growth through their effects on individuals' consumption and saving decisions and investment spending by businesses. Be sure to understand the different multiplier effects and be able to distinguish between discretionary fiscal policy and automatic fiscal policy stabilizers. Understand the lags involved in the implementation and eventual effects of discretionary fiscal policy decisions.

FISCAL POLICY, BUDGET DEFICITS, AND BUDGET SURPLUSES

Fiscal policy refers to the federal government's use of spending and taxation to meet macroeconomic goals. The federal budget is said to be *balanced* when tax revenues equal federal government expenditures. A *budget surplus* occurs when government tax revenues exceed expenditures, and a *budget deficit* occurs when government expenditures exceed tax revenues. The Administration, through action of the President and Congress, enact fiscal policy designed to stabilize the economy. In order to smooth economic cycles, taxes are increased and/or government spending reduced during inflationary periods, and taxes are decreased and/or government spending increased during recessionary periods.

LOS 26.a: Explain supply side effects on employment, potential GDP, and aggregate supply, including the income tax and taxes on expenditure, and describe the Laffer curve and its relation to supply side economics.

Supply-side effects refer to the influence that fiscal policy, especially taxation, has on long-run aggregate supply (potential real GDP). Income taxes reduce the incentive to work by creating a **tax wedge** between pretax and after-tax wages. An increase in income taxes causes after-tax wages to fall. Consequently, workers will be less likely to work the same number of hours as they did when their after-tax wages were higher. As income taxes rise, the full-employment supply of labor (a key factor of production) falls, which reduces potential GDP. These effects are illustrated in Figure 1.

Figure 1: Taxes and Potential GDP

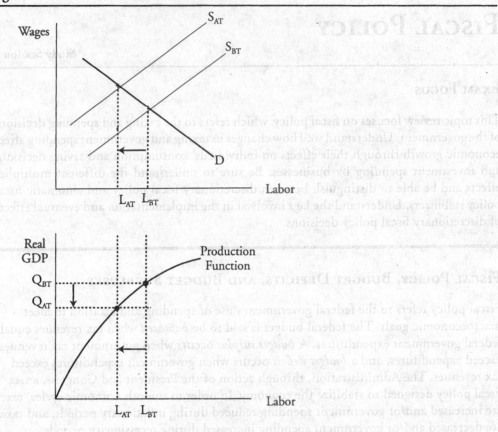

Figure 1 illustrates the link between tax rates and real GDP. The tax increase causes the labor supply curve to shift to the left, from the before-tax supply curve S_{BT} to after-tax supply curve S_{AT}, which reflects a decrease in after-tax income from an hour's work. This results in a drop in the equilibrium (full-employment) quantity of labor from L_{BT} (labor hours before tax) to L_{AT} (labor hours after tax). Real GDP drops as a result of the decrease in the equilibrium quantity of labor. The production function in Figure 1 shows real GDP (the output of the economy adjusted for price level changes) as a function of labor. Potential real GDP supplied decreases from Q_{BT} to Q_{AT} because the quantity of labor supplied at full employment has decreased.

An increase in taxes on consumption expenditures (e.g., sales tax) also causes the supply of labor and potential real GDP to decrease. Workers "convert" hours of work into purchases of goods and services. An increase in expenditure taxes decreases the amount of goods and services that each hour of labor can buy. This disincentive to work reduces the supply of labor, which causes potential GDP to fall.

The Laffer Curve

Because of the supply-side effect on potential GDP, an increase in tax rates will not always result in an increase in tax revenue. Beyond a certain point, the increase in taxes per dollar earned will be more than offset by the decrease in the total number of dollars earned. Economist Arthur Laffer illustrated this relationship in what is called the **Laffer curve.**

Figure 2 shows the Laffer curve. When the tax rate is low, increasing the rate increases total tax revenue. At higher tax rates, however, the supply-side reduction in potential GDP is greater, and the increase in total tax revenue in response to higher tax rates slows. Beyond some rate of taxation (labeled t_m in Figure 2), increasing the tax rate reduces economic output so much that total tax revenues actually decrease.

Much of the debate about "supply-side" fiscal policy recommendations concerns how high the revenue-maximizing tax rate really is, and whether the current tax rate is above or below it.

 Professor's Note: A Laffer curve begins and ends at zero tax revenues. At a 0% tax rate, potential GDP is maximized but no taxes are collected. At a 100% tax rate, tax revenue is zero because potential GDP is zero—no one is willing to supply labor.

Figure 2: Laffer Curve

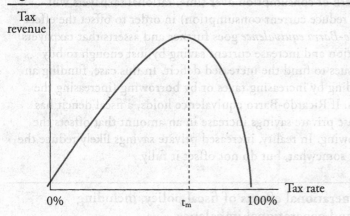

LOS 26.b: Discuss the sources of investment finance and the influence of fiscal policy on capital markets, including the crowding-out effect.

Total investment is one of the major components of GDP (the others are consumption, government spending, and net exports). Investment is defined as expenditures for fixed productive assets and inventory. The **sources of financing for investment** are (1) national savings, (2) borrowing from foreigners, and (3) government savings.

The first two components are private sources of financing. The third source, government savings, equals the difference between government tax revenues and expenditures. Government budget surpluses (savings) increase the sources of total investment, but government budget deficits (borrowing rather than saving) decrease them.

Investment directly affects the growth rate in real GDP. As investment declines, less capital is created, causing the growth rate in real GDP to fall. Conversely, as investment rises, more capital is created, causing the growth rate in real GDP to rise. This is analogous to capital expenditures of a corporation. Corporations invest in capital to increase output.

Fiscal policy decisions (government taxing and spending decisions) have significant impacts on markets for investment capital. Taxes on capital income affect the quantity of savings and investment, leading to changes in real GDP growth. The incentive to save falls as taxes imposed on capital income rise (after-tax returns on savings fall). Therefore, as taxes on capital income rise, private savings likely will fall.

Fiscal policy also affects the supply of government savings. Just as budget surpluses represent government saving, budget deficits require government borrowing (negative saving or dissaving). Larger budget deficits decrease the quantity of savings, which increases the real interest rate, leading firms to reduce their borrowing of financial capital and their investment in physical capital. This adverse effect of a budget deficit on private investment in capital is referred to as the **crowding-out effect**. The decrease in the growth rate of capital will reduce potential GDP.

It may be, however, that increases in the fiscal deficit indirectly cause the amount of private savings to increase. The **Ricardo-Barro effect** refers to the fact that increases in the current deficit mean greater taxes in the future. It is claimed that in order to maintain their preferred pattern of consumption over time, rational taxpayers will increase current savings (and reduce current consumption) in order to offset the effect of higher future taxes. *Ricardo-Barro equivalence* goes further and asserts that taxpayers will reduce current consumption and increase current saving by just enough to buy the bonds the government issues to fund the increased deficit. In this case, funding an increase in government spending by increasing taxes or by borrowing (increasing the deficit) are equivalent actions. If Ricardo-Barro equivalence holds, a fiscal deficit has no crowding-out effect because private savings increase in an amount that offsets the increase in government borrowing. In reality, increased private savings likely reduce the impact of fiscal crowding out somewhat, but do not offset it fully.

LOS 26.c: Discuss the generational effects of fiscal policy, including generational accounting and generational imbalance.

Generational effects of fiscal policy refer to the effects of postponing fiscal imbalances, defined as the present value of future expected government deficits. Eventually, the fiscal imbalance must be corrected by increasing taxes or decreasing government spending. Studies that use **generational accounting** to measure the taxes owed by, and the benefits owed to, each generation show that over half of the fiscal imbalance will be paid by future generations.

The major source of the fiscal imbalance in the United States is payments for Medicare. Since the costs of funding Medicare expenditures are not supported by current federal taxes, the burden of these expenditures will fall on taxpayers in the future. This is a **generational imbalance**; the present value of government benefits to the current generation is not fully paid by the taxes levied on the current generation. In effect, current policy is to postpone the payment of taxes so the burden of government expenditures (to pay for current promises) falls on a future generation (one that isn't able to vote yet!).

LOS 26.d: Discuss the use of fiscal policy to stabilize the economy, including the effects of the government expenditure multiplier, the tax multiplier, and the balanced budget multiplier.

Discretionary fiscal policy refers to the spending and taxing decisions of a national government that are intended to stabilize the economy. (By contrast, **automatic fiscal policy** refers to government spending changes that occur when economic growth slows or accelerates, but do not require action by policy makers.) During recessions, actions can be taken to increase government spending and/or decrease taxes. Either change tends to strengthen the economy by increasing aggregate demand, putting more money in the hands of corporations and consumers to invest and spend. During inflationary economic expansions, actions can be taken to decrease government spending and/or increase taxes. Either change tends to slow the economy by decreasing aggregate demand, taking money out of the hands of corporations and consumers, causing both investment and consumption spending to fall.

Changes in government spending, taxation, or both have magnified effects on aggregate demand. If government spending is increased, aggregate demand increases by a greater amount. This is because the increase in government spending generates additional income, which leads to increases in consumption and investment, which in turn further increases aggregate demand and incomes. The **government expenditure multiplier** refers to the magnitude of the eventual impact on aggregate demand per dollar of change in government spending. The multiplier effect applies equally to increases and decreases in government spending.

Changes in taxes also have a magnified effect on aggregate demand. A decrease in taxes that is not offset by a change in government spending will increase consumption expenditures and thereby increase aggregate demand. This increases incomes, which further increases aggregate demand, which leads to higher incomes, just as an increase in government spending would. Since some of the initial increase in incomes from the tax cut will be saved, and only a percentage spent on increased consumption, the **autonomous tax multiplier** is smaller than the government expenditure multiplier. An increase in taxes will decrease both consumption and savings and will have a magnified effect on aggregate demand as well.

Since the government expenditure multiplier is greater than the tax multiplier, the **balanced budget multiplier** is positive. For an increase in government spending that is accompanied by an equal increase in taxes, the increase in aggregate demand from the spending increase is greater than the decrease in aggregate demand from the tax increase, once their different multiplier effects are considered. The result is that an increase in government spending coupled with an equal increase in taxes will tend to increase aggregate demand.

LOS 26.e: Explain the limitations of discretionary fiscal policy, and differentiate between discretionary fiscal policy and automatic stabilizers.

Discretionary fiscal policy is not an exact science. First, economic forecasts might be wrong, leading to incorrect policy decisions. Second, complications arise in practice that delay both the implementation and resulting effect on the economy of changes in fiscal policy.

- *Recognition delay.* Discretionary fiscal policy decisions are made by the President and voted on by Congress. The state of the economy is complex and it may take the Administration time to recognize the extent of the economic problems.
- *Administrative or law-making delay.* The Administration and Congress cannot vote and enact decisions overnight. Legal changes are delayed while elected officials debate the issues.
- *Impact delay.* Time passes before the effects of the fiscal policy changes are felt. Delays occur in implementing increases and decreases in government spending and taxing. Moreover, it takes time for corporations and individuals to act on the fiscal policy changes.

In contrast to discretionary fiscal policy stabilizers, **automatic stabilizers** are built-in fiscal devices triggered by the state of the economy. Automatic fiscal stabilizers minimize timing problems encountered by discretionary fiscal policy stabilizers. Automatic fiscal stabilizers fall into two main categories: induced taxes and needs-tested spending.

- *Induced taxes* refer to the amount of taxes collected as a percentage (i.e., income tax rate) of income. Incomes are positively related to GDP. Incomes rise during an economic boom. As incomes rise, the total amount of taxes collected automatically increases. The increase in taxes paid by corporations and individuals slows down the economy. Conversely, incomes fall during a recession. As incomes fall, the total amount of taxes collected automatically falls. The decline in taxes paid by corporations and individuals stimulates the economy.
- *Needs-tested spending* refers to government expenditures for programs that pass a "needs" test, such as unemployment. During a recession, unemployment is high. The government automatically pays out more in unemployment compensation. The increase in unemployment compensation stimulates the economy. During an expansion, unemployment payments automatically drop. The decline in unemployment compensation dampens the economy.

Together, induced taxes and needs-tested spending offer automatic stability to the economy. Both actions are countercyclical: taxes rise and needs-based spending falls during expansions, and taxes fall and needs-based spending rises during recessions.

As a result of these automatic fiscal policy effects, the government budget deficit or surplus is affected by the stage of the business cycle. We can think of any budget surplus or deficit as consisting of a structural component and a cyclical component. The **structural surplus or deficit** would still exist if the economy were at full employment. The **cyclical surplus or deficit** exists because the economy is producing above or below full-employment GDP. The cyclical surplus or deficit is zero when real GDP equals potential GDP. The actual surplus or deficit at any point in time equals the sum of any structural surplus or deficit and any cyclical surplus or deficit. Over the last few decades, the U.S. government has had a persistent structural deficit.

 Professor's Note: The automatic stabilizers mentioned here are based on the U.S. tax law and entitlement programs.

KEY CONCEPTS

LOS 26.a

An increase in taxes, whether they are imposed on income or on expenditures, reduces the incentive to work, which decreases the quantity of labor supplied and thereby reduces potential GDP from the supply side.

The Laffer curve illustrates the idea that at some tax rate, the disincentive to work from higher tax rates outweighs the revenue-raising effects of higher tax rates, so that total tax revenue will actually fall in response to a further increase in the tax rate.

LOS 26.b

The sources of investment in an economy are national savings, borrowing from abroad, and government savings.

Government budget surpluses increase total investment funds. Government budget deficits decrease the quantity of savings, which increases the real interest rate, leading firms to reduce investment in physical capital. This is known as the crowding-out effect.

Increased taxes on capital income make saving less attractive, which decreases investment and the long-run growth rate of real GDP.

LOS 26.c

Generational effects of fiscal policy refer to the effects of postponing the taxes necessary to pay for currently enacted federal programs, shifting the burden of paying for unfunded programs to a future generation of taxpayers.

LOS 26.d

The government expenditure multiplier and tax multiplier are measures of the magnified effects of changes in government spending and changes in taxes on aggregate demand. The government expenditure multiplier is greater than the tax multiplier, so that an increase in government spending, together with an equal increase in taxes, tends to increase aggregate demand. This effect is termed the balanced budget multiplier and it is positive.

LOS 26.e

Discretionary fiscal policy changes are intended to smooth economic cycles but are difficult to time correctly because of a recognition lag, while the government identifies the appropriate policy change; a law-making lag, during which fiscal policy changes are enacted; and an impact lag, the time it takes for policy changes to take effect and influence economic activity.

Induced taxes and needs-tested spending are automatic fiscal stabilizers which reduce timing problems because they tend to increase spending and reduce taxes (increase the deficit) during recessions and decrease spending and increase taxes (reduce the deficit) during economic expansions.

CONCEPT CHECKERS

1. Which of the following statements regarding the economic effects of taxes is *most likely* correct?
    A. An increase in income taxes creates an incentive to work more hours.
    B. Decreasing the income tax rate increases the long-term growth rate of the economy.
    C. Taxing consumption instead of income would eliminate the negative effect of taxes on economic growth.

2. The Laffer curve shows that an increase in the tax rate:
    A. will increase total tax revenue.
    B. will decrease total tax revenue.
    C. can either increase or decrease total tax revenue.

3. Which of the following factors is *least likely* to reduce the level of investment?
    A. Lower savings rates.
    B. Federal budget surpluses.
    C. Increased taxes on capital income.

4. Sales in the retail sector have been sluggish and consumer confidence has recently declined, indicating fewer planned purchases. In response, the President sends an expansionary government spending plan to Congress. The plan is submitted on March 30, and Congress refines and approves the terms of the spending plan on June 30. What type of fiscal plan is being considered, and what type of delay did the plan experience between March 30 and June 30?

	Fiscal plan	Type of delay
A.	Automatic	Recognition delay
B.	Automatic	Law-making delay
C.	Discretionary	Law-making delay

5. Congress is concerned about delays in the effects of fiscal policy, and is considering requiring the compilation and reporting of economic statistics weekly, rather than quarterly. The new reporting period is intended to decrease the:
    A. impact delay.
    B. law making delay.
    C. recognition delay.

6. Assume Congress recently enacted an increase in income tax rates on all income levels at a time when the economy was at full-employment GDP. As a result of the tax increase, what are the *most likely* changes in the quantity of labor supplied and potential GDP?

	Quantity of labor	Potential GDP
A.	Increases	Decreases
B.	Decreases	Increases
C.	Decreases	Decreases

7. Congress enacts a program to subsidize farmers in the Midwest with an
    expansive spending program of $10 billion. At the same time, Congress enacts a
    $10 billion tax increase. Which of the following *best* describes the impact on the
    economy?
    A. Lower growth due to the negative tax multiplier.
    B. Higher growth due to the net positive balanced budget multiplier.
    C. No effect on growth because the tax and spending multiplier effects offset.

ANSWERS – CONCEPT CHECKERS

1. **B** Income taxes reduce the incentive to work. Decreasing income taxes encourages workers to work more hours, which increases potential GDP. Consumption taxes also create a disincentive to work because they reduce the amount of goods and services an hour of labor is worth.

2. **C** The Laffer curve shows that at low tax rates an increase in rates will increase total tax revenue, but beyond some rate, further increases will actually decrease total tax revenue.

3. **B** Federal budget surpluses represent government savings, a source from which investment can increase.

4. **C** The expansionary plan initiated by the President and approved by Congress is an example of discretionary fiscal policy. The lag from the time of the submission (March 30) through time of the vote (June 30) is known as law-making delay. It took Congress three months to write and pass the necessary laws.

5. **C** More frequent and current economic data would make it easier for authorities to monitor the economy and to recognize problems. The reduction in the time lag between economic reports would reduce the recognition delay.

6. **C** The increase in income taxes shifts the labor supply curve to the left, resulting in a lower equilibrium quantity of labor. Labor is one of the input factors of production for the economy. Therefore, the lower quantity of labor causes potential GDP to fall.

7. **B** The amount of the spending program exactly offsets the amount of the tax increase, leaving the budget unaffected. The multiplier effect is stronger for government spending than for the tax increase. Therefore, the multiplier will be positive. All of the government spending enters the economy as increased expenditure, whereas only a portion of the tax increase results in lessened expenditure.

MONETARY POLICY

EXAM FOCUS

The material covered here is quite important, as even a casual reader of financial and economic news knows. You should understand that central banks have a mandate to maintain stable prices and that some, such as the U.S. Federal Reserve Bank, have an additional mandate to promote full employment. The other important information here concerns how the Fed determines the appropriate monetary policy, how they implement policy changes, and how these changes actually affect economic activity.

LOS 27.a: Discuss the goals of U.S. monetary policy and the Federal Reserve's (Fed's) means for achieving the goals, including how the Fed operationalizes those goals.

The goals of the U.S. Federal Reserve Bank (the Fed) are three-fold: (1) maximum employment (i.e., maximum sustainable growth of the economy); (2) stable prices; and (3) moderate long-term interest rates.

According to the most recent version of the law establishing the mandate of the Fed (2000 amendments), these goals are to be achieved by maintaining "...long-run growth of the monetary and credit aggregates commensurate with the economy's long-run potential to increase production." Note that the viewpoint here is based on the quantity theory of money and represents a monetarist view of macroeconomics. If money, defined as the money supply and available credit, grows annually at a rate just 1% or 2% higher than the annual growth rate of real output, inflation should average 1% or 2% over the long term.

The goal of moderate long-term interest rates is closely tied to the goal of stable prices, since nominal interest rates are real rates plus expected inflation. Over the long term, most macroeconomists believe that stable prices (which translate typically to inflation of 1% to 2%) and the stability and predictability they bring are an important means of promoting maximum sustainable long-term growth of economic production and employment.

To operationalize its goals, the Fed focuses primarily on two things: core inflation and the difference between actual and potential (full-employment) economic output. Core inflation is calculated as the rate of increase in the Consumer Price Index (CPI) with the effect of its most volatile components (food and energy prices) removed. An adjustment is typically also made for the upward bias that many believe is a result of the way in which the CPI is calculated. While the calculation of the potential or full-employment rate of growth of real GDP is beyond the scope of this review, we do know that the *output gap* between the actual growth rate and the potential growth rate of real GDP is an important consideration in setting monetary policy.

When the output gap is positive (actual > potential), there are inflationary pressures, and a reduction in the money credit aggregates is indicated. When the output gap is negative (actual < potential), we have a *recessionary gap,* and an expansion of money and credit aggregates is indicated.

LOS 27.b: Describe how the Fed conducts monetary policy and explain the Fed's decision-making strategy, including an instrument rule, a targeting rule, open-market operations, and the market for reserves.

The primary way that the Fed conducts monetary policy is through their influence on the **federal funds rate**, the interest rate that banks charge each other for overnight loans of reserves. As with most other central banks, this short-term rate is the Fed's choice of a policy instrument. When the Fed wants to increase the money supply, they decrease their target value for the federal funds rate. When they want to decrease the money supply (or the rate of growth of the money supply), the Fed increases their target value for the federal funds rate.

In determining how to adjust the federal funds rate, the Fed must decide between two types of rules, **instrument rules** and **targeting rules**. When following an instrument rule, the monetary authorities base their target federal funds rate on the current performance of the economy. The **Taylor rule** is an instrument rule based on the rate of inflation and on the output gap. Created by Prof. John Taylor of Stanford University, one version of the Taylor rule, with an inflation target of 2%, sets the federal funds rate as:

$$FFR = 2\% + \text{actual inflation} + 0.5\,(\text{actual inflation} - 2\%) + 0.5\,(\text{output gap})[1]$$

Note that when there is no output gap and inflation is at its target rate of 2%, the FFR is set at 4%. When inflation is above 2% and/or there is a positive (inflationary) output gap, the FFR is increased, and when inflation is below 2% and/or there is a negative (recessionary) output gap, the FFR is decreased. While the Fed does not explicitly follow this rule, it has proven to be a fair approximation of the Fed's policy over the last 20 years.

A targeting rule is based on a forecast of future inflation and requires that the FFR be set so that the forecast of inflation is equal to the target inflation rate, typically 2%.

Since the FFR is determined by supply and demand in the market for interbank loans of reserves, the Fed influences the FFR by increasing or decreasing reserves, primarily through **open market operations**. Open market operations are the buying or selling of Treasury securities by the Fed in the open market. When the Fed buys Treasury securities, cash replaces securities in investor accounts, banks have excess reserves, more funds are available for lending, and the FFR decreases to a level where the quantity of reserves demanded equals the new, larger supply of reserves. Sales of securities by the Fed have the opposite effect, reducing bank reserves available for lending, and increasing the FFR. This increase in the FFR decreases the quantity of reserves demanded to match the decreased supply of reserves. This is the Fed's most commonly used tool and is most important in achieving the federal funds target rate.

---

1. Taylor, John B. "Discretion versus Policy Rules in Practice." *Carnegie-Rochester Conference Series on Public Policy* 39 (1993): 195–214.

LOS 27.c: Discuss monetary policy's transmission mechanism (chain of events) between changing the federal funds rate and achieving the ultimate monetary policy goal when fighting either inflation or recession, and explain loose links and time lags in the adjustment process.

We now turn our attention to how a change in the FFR affects the economy in such a way to achieve the Fed's policy goals regarding GDP growth, employment, and inflation. Let's trace the effects of a decrease in the FFR to stimulate economic activity and growth.

1. The Fed engages in open market purchases of Treasury securities, which increases bank reserves.

2. Excess reserves lead to a decrease in the FFR as banks are more willing to lend reserves to each other.

3. Other short-term rates, such as the T-bill rate, decrease as well since lending reserves and buying T-bills (lending to the U.S. Treasury) are close substitutes. Other interest rates in the economy decrease as well, as banks have more reserves and are more willing to make loans to consumers and businesses. We describe this as the *market for loanable funds*; as the supply of loanable funds increases, the equilibrium rate for loans decreases.

4. Longer-term interest rates, which can be viewed as short-term rates plus a premium for expected inflation, decrease as well.

5. The decrease in rates makes investment in other countries relatively more attractive, reducing the demand for U.S. dollars (for investment), which causes the dollar to depreciate relative to other currencies (more dollars per foreign currency unit).

6. The decrease in interest rates on business loans causes businesses to find borrowing to fund expansion more attractive and spend more on investment in plant and equipment.

7. Consumers react to the reduction in the interest rates on consumer loans by increasing their purchases of goods that are typically financed, such as houses, automobiles, and appliances.

8. The depreciation of the dollar makes U.S. goods prices fall in terms of foreign currency, so foreigners increase their purchases of U.S. goods (i.e., demand for exports increases).

9. In sum, the increases in business investment, consumer purchases of durable goods, and exports all tend to increase aggregate demand.

10. The increase in aggregate demand puts upward pressure on both the price level (increasing inflation) and employment and real GDP.

This whole transmission mechanism, by which decreases in the federal funds rate stimulate aggregate demand and economic growth, is the same but in the opposite direction for an increase in the federal funds rate, which decreases aggregate demand, GDP growth, and inflationary pressure.

In practice, monetary policy actions do not always have their intended effects. There is only a loose link between short-term interest rates, which the Fed can influence directly, and long-term rates, which affect economic decisions by consumers and businesses. A decrease in the FFR will not reduce long-term rates as much if the policy change causes inflation expectations to increase.

Also, monetary policy affects the economy with a significant time lag. By the time an increase in money supply growth to stimulate a recessionary economy actually shows its intended effects, the economy may already be in an expansionary phase. The same holds true, of course, for decisions to reduce money supply growth to slow an inflationary expansion. In either case, the result of the policy changes can actually make economic cycles more severe.

> *Professor's Note: Make sure you can trace the effects of an increase in the federal funds rate from the open market operations of the Fed through to a decrease in aggregate demand and a slowing of economic growth.*

> *Also note that we typically describe the Fed as having three policy tools: the discount rate at which the Fed loans reserves directly to member banks, open market operations, and the bank reserve requirement. When there is a policy change and the Fed increases or decreases the federal funds target rate, they typically change the discount rate similarly at the same time as they pursue the appropriate purchases or sales in their open market operations. The bank minimum reserve requirement is seldom changed.*

LOS 27.d: Describe alternative monetary policy strategies and explain why they have been rejected by the Fed.

There are four alternative rules to the Taylor rule and the policy of targeting the federal funds rate as the key policy variable.

1. A rule called the *McCallum rule* focuses on the rate of growth of the monetary base, based on the quantity theory of money (MV = PY). The rule essentially matches the growth rate of the monetary base to the long-term growth rate of real GDP, adds the target inflation rate, and adjusts for changes in the velocity of money over time. The main drawback of this policy is that fluctuations in the demand for money can cause variations in interest rates that lead to fluctuations in aggregate demand.

2. A rule targeting the rate of growth of the money supply is closely associated with the work of Nobel Laureate Milton Friedman and the quantity theory of money. Friedman's well-known prescription for monetary policy is to grow the money supply at the rate of increase of potential real GDP. The drawbacks of targeting monetary aggregates, which was followed to a large degree in the 1970s when the Fed targeted the growth rates of M1 and M2, are that fluctuations in both the velocity of money and the demand for money can lead to interest rate swings and consequent variability in aggregate demand for goods and services.

3. A rule targeting the exchange rate suggests that money supply growth should be adjusted so that the exchange rate between a country's currency and some basket or index of the currencies of other countries remains stable. In this case, the resulting inflation rate would be that of the other countries in the long term, and the monetary authorities would have little control over it.

4. The final alternative is **inflation targeting**, which is practiced by many central banks with the notable exceptions of Japan and the United States. Under this rule, the central bank makes its inflation expectations explicit and uses open market operations and manages the overnight rate in such a way as to bring expected inflation into line with the target rate, typically 2% with an acceptable range of 1% to 3%. The advantage of this policy rule is predictability and transparency along with the stable expectations for future inflation that result from a central bank's credible commitment to stable prices (the target rate of inflation). Whether inflation targeting would have produced better results in terms of stable prices and economic growth than the targeting based on some variant of the Taylor rule is still an open question and subject to ongoing debate.

> *Professor's Note: Inflation targeting is also discussed in the next topic review on central banks. Note that even in the face of the slowdown in economic activity associated with the collapse of the U.S. housing market, the problems with sub-prime mortgage securities defaults in 2007–2008, and the consequent risk of slowing economic growth and possible recession, the European Central Bank continued to make monetary policy decisions based only on data on current and expected inflation. Time will tell whether inflation targeting produces a better result than the U.S. policy, which has leaned more toward economic stimulus to reduce the probability and/or magnitude of a recession.*

KEY CONCEPTS

LOS 27.a

The goals of the Federal Reserve are to promote full employment, stable prices, and moderate long-term interest rates. The Fed's mandate is to achieve these goals by keeping the long-term growth rate of the monetary aggregates consistent with the potential long-term growth rate of GDP.

The Fed operationalizes its goals by focusing on the core rate of inflation in consumer prices and the difference between potential and actual real GDP growth.

LOS 27.b

The Fed conducts monetary policy primarily by influencing the federal funds rate, the rate at which member banks make overnight loans of reserves to each other.

Under an instrument rule, such as the Taylor rule, the target federal funds rate is based on the current performance of the economy. Under a targeting rule, the target federal funds rate is chosen so as to keep the expected future inflation rate equal to the target rate of inflation.

The Fed uses open market operations to influence the federal funds rate (FFR). In order to decrease (increase) the FFR, the Fed buys (sells) Treasury securities in the open market, which increases (decreases) bank reserves, the money supply, and the supply of loanable funds.

LOS 27.c

The transmission mechanism through which changes in the FFR affect the economy can be described as follows:

1. The Fed buys (sells) Treasury securities, which increases (decreases) bank reserves.
2. The FFR decreases (increases) as banks are more (less) willing to lend each other reserves.
3. Other short-term rates decrease (increase) as the increase (decrease) in the supply of loanable funds decreases (increases) the equilibrium rate for loans.
4. Longer-term interest rates also decrease (increase).
5. The decrease (increase) in rates causes the dollar to depreciate (appreciate) in the foreign exchange market.
6. The decrease (increase) in long-term rates increases (decreases) business investment in plant and equipment.
7. Lower (higher) interest rates cause consumers to increase (decrease) their purchases of houses, autos, and durable goods.
8. Depreciation (appreciation) of the dollar increases (decreases) foreign demand for U.S. exports.
9. These increases (decreases) in consumption, investment, and net exports all increase (decrease) aggregate demand.
10. The increase (decrease) in aggregate demand increases (decreases) inflation, employment, and real GDP.

©2010 Kaplan, Inc.

The link between changes in the FFR and changes in long-term interest rates is actually rather loose, and monetary policy changes only affect the economy with a time lag. As a result, policy decisions do not always have their intended effects at appropriate times.

LOS 27.d

Alternative monetary policy strategies not currently used by the Fed include:

- The McCallum rule, which is focused on the growth rate of the monetary base. Its main drawback is that shifts in the demand for money can cause fluctuations in interest rates and aggregate demand.
- A rule that targets the growth rate of the money supply may also present problems in that changes in both money demand and money velocity can cause volatility in aggregate demand and interest rates.
- Conducting monetary policy to keep the foreign exchange rate with other countries' currencies stable would cause the domestic inflation rate to match that of the other countries, over which the Fed has no control.
- Inflation rate targeting is used by many central banks, the notable exceptions being those of the United States and Japan. The performance of strict inflation targeting, compared to the Fed's method of monetary policy determination, is still subject to debate.

CONCEPT CHECKERS

1. The Federal Reserve's policy goals *least likely* include:
   A. price stability.
   B. minimizing long-term interest rates.
   C. maximizing the sustainable growth rate of the economy.

2. The Fed operationalizes its goals by focusing on:
   A. core inflation and the output gap.
   B. expected inflation and U.S. dollar exchange rates.
   C. food and energy prices and the growth rate of real GDP.

3. The Fed conducts monetary policy primarily by targeting the:
   A. inflation rate.
   B. federal funds rate.
   C. 10-year Treasury note yield.

4. Implementing monetary policy in such a way as to keep the forecast rate of
   inflation at a certain level is *best* described as a(n):
   A. Taylor rule.
   B. instrument rule.
   C. targeting rule.

5. Purchases of Treasury securities in the open market by the Fed are *least likely* to
   increase:
   A. excess reserves.
   B. the federal funds rate.
   C. cash in investor accounts.

6. An increase in the target federal funds rate will *most likely* lead to an increase in:
   A. business investment in fixed assets.
   B. consumer spending on durable goods.
   C. the foreign exchange value of the U.S. dollar.

7. A strategy designed to match the growth rate of the monetary base to the long-
   term growth rate of real GDP plus the target inflation rate is:
   A. the McCallum rule.
   B. inflation targeting.
   C. exchange rate targeting.

ANSWERS – CONCEPT CHECKERS

1. **B** The Fed's goals include maximum employment, which is interpreted as the maximum sustainable growth rate of the economy; stable prices; and *moderate* (not minimal) long-term interest rates.

2. **A** The Fed focuses on the core rate of inflation (the rate of increase in the CPI excluding food and energy prices) and the output gap (the difference between the actual and potential rates of real GDP growth).

3. **B** The primary method by which the Fed conducts monetary policy is through changes in the target federal funds rate.

4. **C** An inflation targeting rule would call for the Fed to base its decisions on a forecast rate of inflation and to set its federal funds rate target at a level that makes the forecast inflation rate equal its target. With an instrument rule, policy decisions are based on the performance of the economy. The Taylor rule is an example of an instrument rule.

5. **B** Open market purchases by the Fed will *decrease* the federal funds rate by increasing excess reserves that banks can lend to one another and, therefore, their willingness to lend.

6. **C** An increase in the target federal funds rate would also be likely to increase longer-term interest rates, which would cause consumption spending on durable goods and business investment in plant and equipment to decrease. The increase in rates would, however, make foreign investment in the United States more attractive, which would increase demand for U.S. dollars and cause the dollar to appreciate.

7. **A** The McCallum rule is designed to set the growth rate of the monetary base at the long-term growth rate of real GDP plus the target rate of inflation, with an adjustment for changes in the velocity of money.

An Overview of Central Banks

Exam Focus

This review has only two LOS. While it primarily concerns central banks of countries other than the United States, the policy tools and goals of central banks around the world are quite similar. The policy tools of central banks were covered in the previous topic review and are covered again in the Fixed Income topic area. Suffice to say, a candidate should be quite familiar with central bank functions, monetary policy tools, and how the goals of economic growth and price stability sometimes conflict in the short run.

LOS 28.a: Identify the functions of a central bank.

The primary function of central banks is to control a country's money supply. The goals are typically price level stability and maximum sustainable growth of real GDP. Most believe that these goals are compatible in the long run. That is, a low, stable, and predictable rate of price inflation supports maximum economic growth. In the short run, however, actions taken to reduce inflationary pressures in the economy may slow economic growth or even lead to a recession. Central banks of different countries have different mandates, but the differences typically are in how much emphasis is placed on promoting economic growth, since all central banks are required to maintain stable prices, often within some prescribed range.

Central banks also typically issue a country's currency and regulate its banking system.

LOS 28.b: Discuss monetary policy and the tools utilized by central banks to carry out monetary policy.

In the United States, the three **policy tools of the central bank** (the Federal Reserve) are:

1. Banks can borrow funds from the Fed if they have temporary shortfalls in reserves. The **discount rate** is the rate at which banks can borrow reserves from the Fed. A lower rate makes reserves less costly to banks, encourages bank lending, and tends to decrease interest rates. A higher discount rate has the opposite effect, raising interest rates.

2. **Bank reserve requirements** are the percentage of deposits that banks must retain (not loan out). By increasing the percentage of deposits that banks are required to retain as reserves, the Fed effectively decreases the funds that are available for lending. This decrease in the amount available for lending will tend to increase interest rates. A decrease in the percentage reserve requirement will increase the funds available for loans, which tends to decrease interest rates. This tool only works well if banks are willing to lend, and their customers are willing to borrow, the additional funds made available by reducing the reserve requirement.

3. **Open market operations** are the buying or selling of Treasury securities by the Fed in the open market. When the Fed buys securities, cash replaces securities in investor accounts, banks have excess reserves, more funds are available for lending, and interest rates decrease. Sales of securities by the Fed have the opposite effect, reducing cash balances and funds available for lending, and increasing interest rates. This is the Fed's most commonly used tool and is important in achieving the federal funds target rate.

In other countries, the tools are essentially the same, but the names may be different. In the U.K., the interbank rate for overnight loans is referred to as the *repo rate* or *repurchase rate*, and this terminology is common in other countries as well. In Australia, the central bank refers to this rate as the *cash rate*, and in Canada it is referred to simply as the *overnight rate*.

When you read that the U.S. Fed has "decreased interest rates," this typically means that they have reduced the federal funds rate, the average rate at which banks loan reserves to each other, usually overnight. Note that the federal funds rate is a market determined rate. However, the central bank usually decreases the discount rate at the same time. To decrease the federal funds rate, the central bank will increase the money supply, increasing banks' excess reserves and their willingness to lend.

While the central banks of many countries use either the discount rate or the overnight rate as their primary policy tool, the goal is to keep inflation within bounds. Managing the money supply in such a way as to keep inflation within prescribed bounds is termed **inflation targeting.** This is the most common monetary policy goal and over the last 20 years, most countries have moved to inflation targeting. Exceptions are the United States and Japan. The U.S. Fed does not target inflation rates specifically, but has a dual mandate of full employment and stable prices. The Bank of Japan does not specifically target an inflation rate, but faces different problems than other countries in this regard as deflation has been seen as a significant threat in recent years, while inflation that is too high has not.

Countries that target inflation typically have a target of 2% annual inflation with an acceptable range of 1% to 3%. Just as central banks use slightly different interest rates for policy making, they also use different measures of price inflation. All use some measure of changes in consumer prices. However, there are differences based on whether some measure of "core" inflation is used. A measure of core inflation is constructed by taking some of the most volatile components of overall prices, such as food and energy, out of the CPI calculation.

To promote economic growth, central banks can, in theory, simply increase target interest rates when the economy is growing at an unsustainably rapid rate and decrease interest rates when economic growth is deemed too slow. In practice the management of a complex economy in a global context is actually quite difficult. Policy changes designed to promote growth may also increase inflation. Changes in interest rates also affect asset prices, income from saving and lending, investment flows between countries, foreign exchange rates, and import and export levels.

KEY CONCEPTS

LOS 28.a

Central banks manage a country's money supply in order to maintain price stability and, with varying emphasis, promote full employment and maximum sustainable long-term growth of the economy. Central banks also issue a country's currency and regulate its banking system.

LOS 28.b

There are three primary tools that central banks use to carry out monetary policy and affect inflation and the rate of economic growth.

- They can reduce (increase) inflation and the growth rate of the economy through open market operations, selling (buying) government securities in order to increase (decrease) short-term interest rates.
- They can reduce (increase) inflation and the growth rate of the economy by increasing (decreasing) the bank reserve requirement, which will decrease (increase) the money supply and increase (decrease) short-term interest rates.
- They can increase (decrease) the interest rate at which they lend reserves to member banks, which will decrease (increase) banks' willingness to lend and reduce (increase) the money supply.

CONCEPT CHECKERS

1. Which of the following is *least likely* a function of a central bank?
    A. Issuing currency.
    B. Lending money to government agencies.
    C. Keeping inflation within an acceptable range.

2. If the rate of inflation in a country were to fall below the range targeted by its government, the central bank would *most likely*:
    A. sell government securities.
    B. increase the reserve requirement.
    C. decrease the overnight or repo rate.

ANSWERS – CONCEPT CHECKERS

1. **B**   Lending money to government agencies is not typically a function of a central bank. Central bank functions include controlling the country's money supply to keep inflation within acceptable levels and promote a sustainable rate of economic growth, as well as issuing currency and regulating banks.

2. **C**   Decreasing the overnight lending rate would add reserves to the banking system, which would encourage bank lending, expand the money supply, reduce interest rates, and allow GDP growth and the rate of inflation to increase. Selling government securities or increasing the reserve requirement would have the opposite effect, reducing the money supply and decreasing the inflation rate.

12 questions: 18 minutes

1. An analyst is evaluating the degree of competition in an industry and compiles the following information:
    *   Few significant barriers to entry or exit exist.
    *   Firms in the industry produce slightly differentiated products.
    *   Each firm faces a demand curve that is largely unaffected by the actions of other individual firms in the industry.

    The analyst should characterize the competitive structure of this industry as:
    A. oligopoly.
    B. monopoly.
    C. monopolistic competition.

2. Which of the following statements about the behavior of firms in a perfectly competitive market is *least accurate*?
    A. A firm experiencing economic losses in the short run will continue to operate if its revenues are greater than its variable costs.
    B. A firm that is producing less than the quantity for which marginal cost equals the market price would lose money by increasing production.
    C. If firms are earning economic profits in the short run, new firms will enter the market and reduce economic profits to zero in the long run.

3. Assume the market for a good is in equilibrium and supply and demand are neither perfectly elastic nor perfectly inelastic. Will an inefficient allocation of resources always result if production of this good is subsidized or if a quota is placed on output?
    A. Both will always result in an inefficient allocation of resources.
    B. Neither will always result in an inefficient allocation of resources.
    C. Only one of these will always result in an inefficient allocation of resources.

4. Which of the following statements about consumer surplus and producer surplus is *most accurate*?
    A. Economic gains to society are maximized at the price and quantity where consumer surplus and producer surplus are equal.
    B. No producer surplus is realized on the sale of an additional unit of a good if the opportunity cost of producing it is greater than the price received.
    C. A consumer is not willing to buy an additional unit of a good if his consumer surplus from the next unit is less than his consumer surplus from the previous unit.

5. Other things equal, an increase of 2.0% in the price of Product X results in a 1.4% increase in the quantity demanded of Product Y and a 0.7% decrease in the quantity demanded of Product Z. Which statement about products X, Y and Z is *least accurate*?
    A. Products Y and Z are complements.
    B. Products X and Z are complements.
    C. Products X and Y are substitutes.

6. What effect will an increase in the expected rate of inflation *most likely* have on aggregate demand and short-run aggregate supply?
   A. Both will increase.
   B. Both will decrease
   C. One will increase and one will decrease.

7. Thomas Lawson is preparing a policy briefing on the effects of fiscal policy on the long-term growth rate of the economy. He includes the following statements in his briefing:

   Statement 1: Taxing income reduces potential GDP because it decreases labor supply. Taxing consumption instead would increase labor supply because higher prices for goods and services encourage workers to work more hours.

   Statement 2: If Ricardo-Barro equivalence does not hold, government budget deficits decrease potential GDP over time by reducing capital investment.

   Are Lawson's statements correct?
   A. Both of Lawson's statements are correct.
   B. Neither of Lawson's statements is correct.
   C. Only one of Lawson's statements is correct.

8. According to real business cycle theory, economic cycles result from:
   A. changes in the rate of productivity growth.
   B. unexpected changes in aggregate demand.
   C. increases and decreases in business confidence.

9. A decrease in the target U.S. federal funds rate is *least likely* to result in:
   A. a proportionate decrease in long-term interest rates.
   B. depreciation of the U.S. dollar on the foreign exchange market.
   C. an increase in consumer spending on durable goods.

10. For an economy that is initially at full-employment real GDP, an increase in aggregate demand will *most likely* have what effects on the price level and real GDP in the short run?
    A. Both will increase in the short run.
    B. Only one will increase in the short run.
    C. Neither will increase in the short run.

11. Potential real GDP is *least likely* to increase as a result of a(n):
    A. improvement in technology.
    B. decrease in the income tax rate.
    C. increase in the money wage rate.

12. When the economy is operating at full employment, it is *most likely* that:
    A. the unemployment rate is zero.
    B. structural unemployment equals frictional unemployment.
    C. cyclical unemployment is less than frictional unemployment.

SELF-TEST ANSWERS – ECONOMICS

1. **C** Both oligopoly and monopolistic competition are consistent with firms that produce slightly differentiated products. However, with few significant barriers to entry and little interdependence among competitors, the industry does not fit the definition of an oligopoly and would be best characterized as monopolistic competition.

2. **B** A firm that is producing *more* than the quantity where its marginal revenue (the market price in perfect competition) is equal to its marginal cost is losing money on sales of additional units. A firm producing where marginal cost is less than price is foregoing additional profit by not increasing production. The other responses accurately describe characteristics of firms in perfectly competitive markets.

3. **C** A subsidy to producers will shift the supply curve to the right and increase the quantity supplied of this good to a level greater than the equilibrium quantity. Resources that have greater value in other uses will be diverted to producing this good, so a loss of economic efficiency results. A production quota will cause a loss of efficiency only if the quota level is less than the original equilibrium quantity.

4. **B** Producers realize a producer surplus on the next unit of a good when the price they receive for it is greater than the opportunity cost of producing it. Economic gains to society are greatest when the sum of consumer surplus and producer surplus is maximized, regardless of which is larger. A consumer is willing to buy an additional unit of a good as long as it will generate *any* additional consumer surplus.

5. **A** It does not necessarily follow from the information given in the question that products Y and Z are complements.

   The increase in the price of Product X caused the quantity demanded of Product Y to increase (positive cross elasticity) and caused the quantity demanded of Product Z to decrease (negative cross elasticity). This suggests that Product Y is a substitute for Product X, and Product Z is a complement to Product X.

   But this does not mean Product Y is a complement to Product Z. For example, gasoline is a complement to automobiles; bicycles are a substitute for automobiles; but gasoline is not a complement to bicycles.

6. **C** Increases in expected inflation lead to higher money wage demands, which causes a decrease in short-run aggregate supply (SAS curve shifts up). Higher expected inflation will also encourage consumers to make purchases sooner than they otherwise would have and increase future expected business profits and, consequently, current business investment, both of which increase aggregate demand (shift the AD curve up).

7. **C** Statement 1 is incorrect. Consumption taxes have the same negative effect on the incentive to work as income taxes. By increasing the cost of goods and services, consumption taxes decrease the real value of an hour of labor and therefore result in less labor input, just as income taxes reduce the amount of real goods and services that can be purchased with a given money wage. Statement 2 is correct. Government deficits cause a "crowding-out" effect on private investment that decreases capital investment and reduces potential GDP. Ricardo-Barro equivalence is the theory that government borrowing causes private savings to increase enough to fund the borrowing, which implies that government borrowing has no crowding-out effect on capital investment.

8. **A**   Real business cycle theory holds that economic cycles are driven by fluctuations in the growth rate of productivity that result from changes in technology. Keynesian cycle theory attributes the business cycle to changes in business confidence, while new classical cycle theory suggests business cycles are driven by unexpected changes in aggregate demand.

9. **A**   Changes in the U.S. federal funds rate and changes in long-term interest rates are unlikely to be proportionate. Long-term rates are the sum of short-term rates and a premium for the expected rate of inflation. If a decrease (increase) in the target federal funds rate by the Fed causes economic agents to increase (decrease) their inflation expectations, the change in long-term rates will be less than the change in the federal funds rate. Increases in spending on consumer durables and a decrease in the foreign exchange value of the U.S. dollar are among the expected results of a decrease in the target U.S. federal funds rate.

10. **A**   An increase in aggregate demand will cause short-run equilibrium to move along the short-run aggregate supply curve (SAS). This will tend to increase both real GDP and the price level in the short run.

11. **C**   An increase in the money wage rate would not increase long-run aggregate supply (potential real GDP), but instead would decrease the short-run aggregate supply curve. An improvement in technology would tend to increase potential real GDP. Decreasing the income tax rate narrows the tax wedge between pretax and after-tax income, which increases the full-employment quantity of labor supplied and potential real GDP.

12. **C**   Cyclical unemployment is zero at full employment, while structural and frictional unemployment are always greater than zero so that total unemployment is greater than zero at full-employment real GDP.

FORMULAS

price elasticity of demand $= \dfrac{\text{percent change in quantity demanded}}{\text{percent change in price}} = \dfrac{\%\Delta Q}{\%\Delta P}$

where: percent change $= \dfrac{\text{change in value}}{\text{average value}} = \dfrac{\text{ending value} - \text{beginning value}}{\left(\dfrac{\text{ending value} + \text{beginning value}}{2}\right)}$

cross elasticity of demand $= \dfrac{\text{percent change in quantity demanded}}{\text{percent change in price of substitute or complement}}$

income elasticity of demand $= \dfrac{\text{percent change in quantity demanded}}{\text{percent change in income}}$

price elasticity of supply $= \dfrac{\text{percent change in quantity supplied}}{\text{percent change in price}} = \dfrac{\%\Delta Q}{\%\Delta P}$

total cost = total fixed cost + total variable cost

marginal cost $= \dfrac{\text{change in total cost}}{\text{change in output}} = \dfrac{\Delta TC}{\Delta Q}$

average fixed cost = TFC / Q

average variable cost = TVC / Q

average total cost = AFC + AVC

unemployment rate $= \dfrac{\text{number of unemployed}}{\text{labor force}} \times 100$

labor force participation rate $= \dfrac{\text{labor force}}{\text{working-age population}} \times 100$

employment-to-population ratio $= \dfrac{\text{number of employed}}{\text{working-age population}} \times 100$

CPI $= \dfrac{\text{cost of basket at current prices}}{\text{cost of basket at base period prices}} \times 100$

$$\text{inflation rate} = \frac{\text{current CPI} - \text{year-ago CPI}}{\text{year-ago CPI}} \times 100$$

aggregate demand = consumption + investment + government spending + net exports

potential deposit expansion multiplier = 1 / (required reserve ratio)

potential increase in money supply = potential deposit expansion multiplier × increase in excess reserves

$$\text{money multiplier} = \frac{(1+c)}{(r+c)}$$

change in quantity of money = change in monetary base × money multiplier

equation of exchange:

money supply × velocity = GDP = price × real output

quantity theory of money:

$$\text{price} = M\left(\frac{V}{Y}\right)$$

INDEX

Notes